# 50 POST WAR SEASONS OF SUNDERLAND AFC

by
Mel
Kirtley

# Acknowledgements

I WISH to thank the management and staff of The Sunderland Echo for their assistance and cooperation with the publication of this book.

In particular, my thanks go to Stuart Bell for supporting the publication of the book. Thanks also go to David Dodds and Mark Dorrian for their assistance in coordinating the numerous preparatory stages of the publication.

The efforts of the Composing, Library, Photographic, Promotions and Reprographic departments are greatly appreciated.

I also wish to acknowledge the assistance of Elizabeth Weightman, Harry Lorraine, Geoff Dickens and Trevor Wood.

Special thanks to Alex Bayley-Kaye.

**Mel Kirtley**
**1996**

*Published by Wearside Books.*

© *Copyright 1996. Wearside Books*

*All photographs are reproduced courtesy of* The Sunderland Echo.

*Cover Design:* Mark Dorrian

**ISBN 0 9525380 2 4**

# Foreword

**R**ESEARCHING the affairs and results of Sunderland A.F.C. over the last fifty years has been a labour of love. I have been a supporter of the club for thirty five of those fifty years and I can honestly say that during that time there has hardly been a dull moment.

Over the fifty years, the club has had more than its fair share of ups and downs. Supporters have been taken from the depths of despair during six relegation seasons, including one to the old Third Division, to the elation of six promotions and four Wembley appearances including the never to be forgotten F.A. Cup triumph of 1973.

Through it all, one factor has remained constant. The fervour and the passion of Sunderland's magnificent supporters who have followed the club week in week out, season after season, through thick and thin.

I hope that the memories of events long gone will come flooding back as you turn the pages of this book and that you will have as much pleasure reliving the past as I have had recalling it.

**Mel Kirtley**
**1996**

*Flyleaf photograph. Ian Porterfield's winning goal for Sunderland in*
*the 1973 F.A. Cup Final.*

*Front cover photographs. Ian Porterfield's goal (1973)*
*Len Shackleton (1948-1959)*
*Marco Gabbiadini (1987-1991)*

# Football Echo

**T**HE Sunderland Football Echo was first published on 7th September 1907. The "Pink 'Un" as it became affectionately known first turned white towards the end of the 1912-1913 season. The colour change was made because of shortages of pink paper but as the first white edition appeared on the night of Sunderland's defeat by Aston Villa in the F.A. Cup Final, many readers said that the Football Echo had turned white with shock!

After the first world war, the Football Echo was printed on blue paper but there were repeated requests from readers to revert to the the traditional pink colour. The Sunderland Echo made a promise that when Sunderland won the cup the flush of victory would be sufficient to turn the Football Echo pink.

The great day arrived on 1st May 1937 when a 3-1 victory over Preston North End at Wembley saw the F.A. Cup return to Roker Park. Copies of the Football Echo were printed at Sunderland and Portsmouth with the latter copies being rushed to London where 20,000 were sold.

The re-appearance of the "Pink 'Un" was a sign that Sunderland had won the F.A. Cup and the Football Echo continued to be printed on pink paper until 26th April 1958 when it again turned white with shock — this time as a result of the club's relegation to the Second Division for the first time in their history.

From the start of the 1958-1959 season, the newspaper was once again printed on blue paper and the Sunderland Echo gave an undertaking that it would not re appear in its familiar pink colour until Sunderland won promotion to the First Division or won the F.A. Cup.

Promotion was secured on 18th April 1964 when Sunderland defeated Charlton Athletic 3-1 at Roker Park and the "Pink 'Un" returned! By now it was an accepted tradition that chapters of the club's history should be marked by the changing colour of the Football Echo.

On Wednesday 15th April 1970, Sunderland's failure to defeat Liverpool at Roker Park sent them crashing back to the Second Division and the following Saturday's edition of the Football Echo was printed on blue paper with the usual promise that the "Pink 'Un" would return as soon as the team were promoted back to the First Division or won the F.A. Cup.

The flush of victory over Leeds United in the F.A. Cup Final at Wembley on 5th May 1973 once again turned the newspaper pink and it continued to be printed on pink paper for the next four years. Defeat by Everton on Thursday 19th May 1977 confirmed Sunderland's relegation to the Second Division and the following Saturday's edition of the Football Echo turned white with shock but, due to reader response, it reverted to pink at the start of the 1977-1978 season.

Following Sunderland's relegation to the Third Division, the Football Echo ceased being printed on pink paper after 16th May 1987. On 1st August 1987, the Football Echo was re-named the Sports Echo and was printed on white paper. By this time, commercial considerations dictated the colour of the paper used and the "Pink 'Un" re-appeared on 6th August 1994 and it has remained pink ever since.

Argus was the pen-name of the Football Echo's sports editor until 1st December 1979. During the period covered by this book, two reporters wrote in the Football Echo as Argus. Jack Anderson covered Sunderland's games as Argus until November 1950 with Bill Butterfield taking over on 2nd December 1950. He continued to cover Sunderland's games until retirement after the game on 24th November 1979. Since then, Geoff Storey has reported on Sunderland's games in the Football Echo and Sports Echo but the name Argus was dropped at the time of Bill Butterfield's retirement.

As sports editor of a major provincial newspaper, Bill Butterfield was entitled to a ticket to the F.A. Cup Final each season but always turned down the privilege, saying that he would only attend if and when Sunderland were playing. His big moment did of course arrive on 5th May 1973!

# SEASON SUMMARY

## 1946-1947

League football re-commenced on 31st August 1946 following the end of wartime hostilities. Sunderland's first game was a home fixture against Derby County which they won 3-2 with goals from Eddie Burbanks and Cliff Whitelum (2).

The season saw several good home wins with victories against Huddersfield Town (3-0), Everton (4-1), Aston Villa (4-1) and Bolton Wanderers (3-1) although there were heavy away defeats at Charlton Athletic (5-0), Portsmouth (4-1), Derby County (5-1) and Aston Villa (4-0).

Sunderland's indifferent away form was continued in the F.A. Cup when they suffered a third round exit at the hands of Second Division Chesterfield, losing 2-1.

**Incoming players included:**
Fred Hall, Arthur Hudgell, Tommy McLain, J.H.K. Oliver, Thomas Reynolds, Jackie Robinson, W. Walsh.

**Outgoing Players included:**
Cyril Brown, Ken Willingham.

**Sunderland's league record read:**

| P | W | D | L | F | A | Pts | Position |
|---|---|---|---|---|---|-----|----------|
| 42 | 18 | 8 | 16 | 65 | 66 | 44 | 9th |

League appearances (with F.A. Cup appearances in brackets): Burbanks 32 (1), Davis 12 (1), Duns 33, Ellison 3, Finlay 1, Hall 25 (1), Housam 33 (1), Hudgell 16, Jones 24 (1), Lindsay 1, Lloyd 19, Mapson 42 (1), McLain 11, Reynolds 12, Robinson 30 (1), Scotson 5, Stelling 40 (1), Walsh 18, Watson 32 (1), White 2, Whitelum 34 (1), Willingham 14, Wright 23 (1).

*Eddie Burbanks joined the club in 1935 and played most of his games for Sunderland in pre-war seasons.*

Average home attendance: 35,364.

The average home attendance is calculated on league and F.A. Cup games only. From season 1960-1961 onwards, League Cup attendances are included in the calculation.

*In the Sunderland Football Echo, Argus' end of season comment read, "Can anyone honestly say that the Sunderland club has any reasonable prospect of gaining honours with the present side. While I can see no improvement unless some players are signed, I hope to be proved wrong. I prefer to look facts squarely in the face and the facts as I see them are that the team will be no better next season than this unless money is wisely spent and that is too dangerous a position for any club to be in unless all the others are standing still too."*

### Division 1 1946-1947 — SUNDERLAND 3    DERBY COUNTY 2

Long before 1.00pm crowds were flocking to Roker Park and by 2.30pm the grandstand gates had been closed to all but season ticket holders. There was a roar of applause when Raich Carter led the Derby players out to face his former club in this, the first post war league game. Carter was very much in the thick of things early in the game with Sunderland's Housam and Hall both coming to the rescue as he raced through towards goal. After ten minutes Sunderland took the lead as Derby's Howe used his arm to control a Duns' centre. Burbanks drove in a low penalty kick to Woodley's right hand to beat the goalkeeper all the way. At the end of 30 minutes, Derby County got on equal terms with a well worked goal by Stamps. Sunderland had been attacking and when the ball was cleared their defence was wide open and Stamps had a clear run on goal. Mapson rushed out of goal but before he could get to the ball, the Derby player pulled it to one side and ran on the place it into the untenanted goal. Just before the interval, Sunderland regained their lead when Watson hooked the ball over the head of a Derby player and Whitelum hit a terrific drive on the half turn which hit the top of the net. The Sunderland Football Echo reported that this leading goal was received with tremendous cheering by the crowd.

The opening of the second half was sensational as Whitelum scored again as he raced through to meet a centre from the right wing. The Derby goalkeeper left his goal to meet Sunderland's centre forward who neatly pushed the ball through Woodley's legs and into the net. Then a fine shot by Carter was knocked over the bar by Mapson and from the resultant corner kick, Jones used his arm to control the ball. Doherty scored from the penalty kick. Towards the end of the game, tempers were becoming frayed and both Carter and Walsh were spoken to by the referee. Just before the final whistle, the ball was sent on to the top of the clock stand and burst. Another ball was thrown in but no sooner had the game restarted than the whistle sounded with Sunderland victors.

**Sunderland:** Mapson, Stelling, Jones, Willingham, Hall, Housam, Lloyd, Watson, Duns, Whitelum, Burbanks.

**Derby County:** Woodley, Howe, Nicholas, Musson, Leuty, Bullions, Doherty, Carter, Morrison, Stamps, Walsh.

# 1947-1948

Sunderland finished the season in their worst position to date; a 3-0 victory over Middlesbrough at Roker Park in the penultimate game of the season saving the team the anxiety of having to go into the final fixture needing a win to ensure First Division survival.

Despite finishing the season in twentieth position, attendances at Roker Park showed a significant increase over the previous season. This was partially due to the fact that the team's home performances were better than their league position suggested. Indeed, twenty six of the team's thirty six points were won at Roker Park.

Once again, a Second Division club prevented Sunderland from progressing beyond the third round of the F.A. Cup. On this occasion the victors were Southampton, winning by the only goal of the game at The Dell.

**Incoming players included:**
Frank Bee, Jimmy McGuigan, B. Ramsden, Len Shackleton, Ronnie Turnbull.

**Outgoing players included:**
Eddie Burbanks, Jack Jones, Ken Walshaw, Thomas White, Cliff Whitelum.

**Sunderland's league record read:**

| P | W | D | L | F | A | Pts | Position |
|----|----|----|----|----|----|-----|----------|
| 42 | 13 | 10 | 19 | 56 | 67 | 36 | 20th |

League appearances (with F.A. Cup appearances in brackets): Bee 5, Burbanks 15 (1), Davis 26 (1), Duns 38 (1), Hall 39 (1), Hetherington 2, Housam 2, Hudgell 40 (1), Lloyd 5, Mapson 41 (1), McGuigan 1, McLain 22 (1), Oliver 4, Quinn 6, Ramsden 2, Reynolds 27, Robinson (J) 22, Robinson (R) 1, Scotson 18, Shackleton 14, Stelling 40 (1), Turnbull 16 (1), Walsh 8, Watson 22 (1), Whitelum 7, Wright 39 (1).

Average home attendance: 42,482.

*Fred Hall was one of Sunderland's first post-war signings when he joined the club from Blackburn Rovers in August 1946.*

*At the end of the season, Argus wrote in the Sunderland Football Echo, "The sad state of affairs which were endured this season will exist again next season unless the weaknesses in the side are quickly remedied. At the beginning of the season, supporters were told that the aim of the club was to gain a reasonable league position in the re-building period. The only improvement in performances were seen in the latter weeks of the season when the team fought hard to save the club from Second Division football. The forward line must receive attention before next season opens. If the Roker directors are satisfied with the right flank, four fifths of the club's supporters are not. In 1939, we were looking for a new outside right. Nine years later, the same player holds the position with no more consistency than he did in 1939."*

**Division 1 1947-1948**  |  **SUNDERLAND 5   LIVERPOOL 1**

Sunderland played some terrific attacking football in the early exchanges with Watson, playing in an experimental centre forward position, prominent for his distribution to either wing. In the 18th minute when Paisley tried a clearance the ball rebounded off Balmer to Davis. The Sunderland man was unmarked and went through to draw the Liverpool goalkeeper to place a weak shot inside the upright. Sunderland went further ahead after 31 minutes when Watson sent the ball out to Duns and then ran into the goalmouth to meet the winger's centre and head through a lovely goal. Just as the referee was about to signal half time, Liverpool's Liddell reduced the arrears to make the half time scoreline 2-1.

In the second half, Quinn met a ball from the right wing and hit a shot which crept under Minshull's body and into the net. Fifteen minutes later Quinn struck again when he hit a ball from well outside the angle of the penalty area which seemed to swerve in the air before dropping into the net. Sunderland completed the scoring when Arthur Wright brought the ball down a few yards from the half way line. He crossed to the right wing where Duns collected the ball and dropped it into the middle of the goal for Davis to head into the net.

**Sunderland:** Mapson, Stelling, Hudgell, McLain, Hall, Wright, Davis, Quinn, Duns, Watson, Burbanks.

**Liverpool:** Minshull, Jones, Lambert, Taylor, Hughes, Paisley, Baron, Balmer, Priday, Stubbins, Liddell.

# 1948-1949

Sunderland suffered something of a goal drought, scoring just forty nine league goals which was the club's worst seasonal haul since membership of the First Division was increased to twenty two clubs in 1920-1921 season.

Despite this, the club finished the season in a creditable eighth position. High spots of the season included two fine wins over Manchester United, eventual championship runners-up that year, as well as convincing home victories over Manchester City (3-0), Chelsea (3-0) and Bolton Wanderers (2 0).

However, it was in the F.A. Cup that Sunderland were to make the headlines and for all the wrong reasons. Following a welcome 2-0 success at Crewe Alexandra, Sunderland were drawn away to Southern League side Yeovil Town. The tiny non league side took a surprise lead but when Jackie Robinson equalised for Sunderland it was thought that it would only be a matter of time before Bill Murray's men made their superiority count. At that time, F.A. Cup games were settled in extra time in the first match and it was during extra time that Yeovil Town scored the winning goal which gave them a 2-1 victory which remains one of the biggest F.A. Cup upsets in the history of the competition.

**Incoming players included:**
Ivor Broadis, Tommy Dougall, Harry Kirtley, Ken Smith, Tommy Wright.

**Outgoing players included:**
Frank Bee, Harry Hetherington, Arthur Housam.

**Sunderland's league record read:**

| P | W | D | L | F | A | Pts | Position |
|---|---|---|---|---|---|-----|----------|
| 42 | 13 | 17 | 12 | 49 | 58 | 43 | 8th |

League appearances (with F.A. Cup appearances in brackets): Broadis 13, Davis 20, Dougall 3, Duns 22 (2), Hall 36 (2), Hudgell 41 (1), Kirtley 3, Mapson 32 (2), McGuigan 2, McLain 1, Oliver 4, Ramsden 10 (1), Reynolds 32 (2), Robinson (J) 29 (2), Robinson (R) 10, Scotson 22, Shackleton 39 (2), Stelling 33 (2), Turnbull 6 (2), Walsh 2, Watson 30 (2), Wright (A) 42 (2), Wright (T) 12.

Average home attendance: 45,118.

*Len Shackleton played for Sunderland over a ten year period during which time he scored 101 goals for the club.*

*Following the final game of the season, a 1-1 home draw with Birmingham City on 7th May, Argus wrote in the Sunderland Football Echo, "Sunderland have at least secured a respectable position in the league. However, too little thought has been given to the strength of the reserve team with the result that certain players think they can play just as they like and get away with it simply because they know that whatever game they put up, there is no one to replace them. Candidly, it is tragic that a team of Sunderland's standing cannot find players much better than they have got playing in the reserve team. With the club finishing in eighth position, criticism is likely to be disarmed and a feeling of smugness overcome everyone. I've not got that feeling and I strongly believe that a couple of players would make Sunderland into a championship proposition."*

# 1949-1950

Sunderland embarked upon a goal scoring spree with a season's return of eighty three goals. This established a post war record which has yet to be beaten in top flight football. Not surprisingly, such attacking football brought its rewards at the turnstiles and for the first and only time in the club's history, the aggregate seasonal attendance at Roker Park topped the one million mark. Two outstanding attendances were for the games against Blackpool (64,888) and Newcastle United (68,004).

Sunderland finished the season in third position, although this respectable achievement was cloaked in disappointment. Following an emphatic 3-0 away victory at Fulham on 8th April, it seemed that league championship honours were destined to come to Roker Park. However, three successive defeats in the last five games soon dashed all hopes of that. Of the three end of season defeats, the most disappointing was the one at home against Manchester City in which the Mancunian's goalkeeper Bert Trautmann saved a twice taken penalty by Jack Stelling. Manchester City were relegated and with Sunderland ending the season with fifty two points Portsmouth won the championship with fifty three points and a better goal average than Wolverhampton Wanderers who shared an identical points haul.

Although for the fourth successive post-war season Sunderland failed to progress beyond the fourth round of the F.A. Cup, they at least experienced the satisfaction of a resounding third round 6-0 home win against Huddersfield Town before losing 5-1 in the next round at White Hart Lane.

**Incoming players included:**
Dave Agnew, Norman Case, A. E. Snell.

**Outgoing players included:**
Jimmy McGuigan, J. H. K. Oliver, Jackie Robinson, B. Ramsden, Ronnie Turnbull.

**Sunderland's league record read:**

| P | W | D | L | F | A | Pts | Position |
|---|---|---|---|---|---|-----|----------|
| 42 | 21 | 10 | 11 | 83 | 62 | 52 | 3rd |

League appearances (with F.A. Cup appearances in brackets): Broadis 41 (2), Case 3, Craig 1, Davis 34 (2), Duns 3, Hall 13, Hudgell 40 (2), Kirtley 5, Mapson 40 (2), McLain 6 (2), Reynolds 42 (2), Robinson (R) 2, Scotson 11, Shackleton 40 (2), Stelling 42 (2), Walsh 29 (2), Watson 32 (2), Wood 1, Wright (A) 35, Wright (T) 42 (2).

Average home attendance: 48,130.

*Tommy Wright in action for Sunderland during the 1949-1950 season.*

*In a strongly worded end of season summary, Argus wrote in the Sunderland Football Echo, "Sunderland could never have had a better chance to win the championship than they did this season. Sunderland do not have a championship defence and the club paid the penalty for not remedying an obvious weakness months ago. This weakness in defence has been detrimental to Willie Watson's international prospects and has meant that he had to do two men's work. Amazingly, Watson has shown so much stamina in his games that he has coped well but there is always a danger under these conditions of burning up stored energy and reducing a man's playing life."*

### F.A. Cup (Third Round) 1949-1950

## SUNDERLAND 6 HUDDERSFIELD TOWN 0

By 8.30am supporters were gathering outside the ground and long queues had formed by the time the gates opened at 12.30pm. There were 55,097 present by kick off although the Roker End was nothing like packed.

Sunderland took the lead after 6 minutes when Shackleton won a tackle and swept the ball to Tommy Wright who centred for Davis to score. Four minutes later Wright was again involved in a goal after his centre was put away by Broadis. It was all Sunderland and incredibly the same combination produced Sunderland's third goal on ten minutes when Wright again provided the opportunity for Broadis to score. Len Shackleton further increased Sunderland's lead after 26 mintues. The ball ran loose for Reynolds to hook across the six yard line and, as it was knee high, Shackleton did not hesitate to shoot and scored a great goal.

Huddersfield's best attacking period was early in the second half but Sunderland were back on the goal trail after 55 minutes. Tommy McLain started an attack on the right and when Tommy Wright centred, Shackleton neatly trapped the ball, manoeuvred for position and beat Mills with a beautiful ground shot.

Sunderland completed the thrashing after 85 minutes when Tommy Wright hit a grand drive which Mills turned against the bar. The ball rebounded to Davis who scored the easiest of goals.

**Sunderland:** Mapson, Stelling, Hudgell, Watson, Walsh, McLain, Broadis, Shackleton, Wright, Davis, Reynolds.

**Huddersfield Town:** Mills, Hayes, Howe, Glazzard, Hepplewhite, Boot, Nightingale, Hassall, McKenna, Burke, Metcalfe.

# 1950-1951

Sunderland signed Trevor Ford from Aston Villa for a record transfer fee of £30,000 and in doing so they assembled what manager Bill Murray and most supporters considered to be the best forward line in Britain. This was Shackleton, Broadis and Ford. In his first home game with the club, a 5-1 win against Sheffield Wednesday, Ford scored a hat trick and also dislodged a post at the Fulwell end!

Despite the justified optimism of the club's supporters and the inclusion of three international players in the side (Watson, Shackleton and Ford), the season was one of disappointment. Sunderland finished in twelfth position in the league and collected forty points.

The season saw F.A. Cup victories against Coventry City, Southampton and Norwich City (all from the lower leagues at the time) but a home tie against Wolverhampton Wanderers in the quarter finals produced only a 1-1 draw. Sunderland lost the replay at Molineux 3-1.

**Incoming players included:**
Billy Bingham, Laurie Bolton, John Bone, Gordon Cunning, Trevor Ford, Jack Hedley.

**Outgoing players included:**
Norman Case, Tommy Dougall, Reg Scotson.

**Sunderland's league record read:**

| P | W | D | L | F | A | Pts | Position |
|---|---|---|---|---|---|-----|----------|
| 42 | 12 | 16 | 14 | 63 | 73 | 40 | 12th |

League appearances (with F.A. Cup appearances in brackets): Agnew 1, Bingham 13, Broadis 20 (3), Case 1, Cunning 5, Davis 24 (5), Duns 9 (2), Ford 26 (5) Hall 15, Hedley 21 (5), Hudgell 41 (5), Kirtley 15, Mapson 41 (5), McLain 17 (3), Reynolds 25, Scotson 5, Shackleton 30 (4), Smith 1, Stelling 22, Walsh 32 (5), Watson 27 (3), Wright (A) 37 (5), Wright (T) 34 (5).

Average home attendance: 41,702.

*Willie Watson played both football and cricket for England. He joined Sunderland from Huddersfield Town in April 1946 and played over two hundred games for the club.*

*Once again, Argus was far from impressed with Sunderland's season as this extract from his notes in the Sunderland Football Echo show. "Another season of First Division membership safely tucked away — with the emphasis on the safety angle! It had its highlights in the shape of a good F.A. Cup run, the best in post war football, and a solid second half of the season effort which dispelled all relegation fears well before the end. However, the facts and figures of the slide which started after the first game are recorded to sound a warning note which club officials cannot afford to ignore. By early December, the yield from twenty one games was only fifteen points and although we should applaud the players who pulled the team clear, the call was closer than it should have been. Four times in five seasons Sunderland have been seriously concerned about their league position and each time it has been a winning race to safety. It may be that the unhappy sequence is at an end and that a brighter run is in the offing. Team building must begin in the close season as the pattern of Sunderland's position next season may well be shaped by close season activity."*

# 1951-1952

The 1951-1952 season was something of a non event. Whilst there were creditable away performances which earned the club twenty points, there were some far from satisfactory displays at Roker Park. Apart from the occasional convincing victory, including a 7-1 drubbing of Huddersfield Town, Sunderland stuttered through their home programme and managed to chalk up only twenty two points all season.

Of the seventy goals scored, forty four of them were credited equally to Ford and Shackleton.

Yet again, there was little joy to be gained from the F.A. Cup with Sunderland losing out to Stoke City in a third round replay.

**Incoming players included:**
George Aitken, Stan Anderson, Ted McNeill, Johnny McSeveney, William Morrison.

**Outgoing players included:**
Ivor Broadis, Gordon Cunning.

**Sunderland's league record read:**

| P | W | D | L | F | A | Pts | Position |
|---|---|---|---|---|---|-----|----------|
| 42 | 15 | 12 | 15 | 70 | 61 | 42 | 12th |

League appearances (with F.A. Cup appearances in brackets): Aitken 23 (2), Bingham 36 (2), Broadis 5, Davis 14, Duns 8, Ford 39 (2), Hall 42 (2), Hedley 26 (2), Hudgell 26 (2), Kirtley 25 (2), Mapson 24, Marston 7, McLain 9, McSeveney 20 (2), Reynolds 8, Robinson 18 (2), Shackleton 41 (2), Stelling 25, Watson 36 (2), Wright (A) 26, Wright (T) 4.

Average home attendance: 40,084.

*Welsh international Trevor Ford joined Sunderland from Aston Villa in 1950 for a then record transfer fee of £30,000.*

*Once again, Argus was unimpressed with Sunderland's season when he wrote, "Another safe season in the bag to add to the illustrious club record of unbroken First Division membership. With it perhaps is the temptation to feel on the evidence of closing games that the side was capable of ensuring that they should not have been in danger of relegation at any stage of the season. That temptation needs resisting however for Sunderland met a string of mediocre clubs after being deservedly beaten by Manchester United and Tottenham Hotspur in successive games. On the season as a whole, the best that can be said is that the club finished where they are entitled to do — in the middle of the table. From the absence of any show of enterprise in the closing weeks of the season, it seems safe to assume that the directors will be quite happy to go forward to next season with the same well tried senior playing staff. The club states that it is out of pocket on the season and that this will put a severe brake on any transfer activity in the top flight of the market."*

# 1952-1953

This was the season when Sunderland managed to cure their indifferent home form. They lost only once all season at Roker Park and that was against Newcastle United in September. Indeed by the time that the third round of the F.A. Cup came around Sunderland were challenging for championship honours.

Further disappointment was experienced in the F.A. Cup with Sunderland making a fourth round exit against Burnley at Turf Moor.

The season was notable for the debut of Stan Anderson who became one of the most talented players to wear a red and white shirt and who served Sunderland with distinction for the best part of twelve seasons.

Despite some superb league performances, including the double over ultimate champions Arsenal, Sunderland's eratic form was giving cause for concern. The team took a mere nine points from the last thirteen games of the season; a run which yielded just two victories. One of these victories was against Cardiff City at Roker Park in the final fixture of the season. The game was watched by 7,469 spectators and it was that statistic which really set the alarm bells ringing.

**Incoming players included:**
Fred Chilton, Leslie Dodds, Sam Kemp, Harry Threadgold.

**Outgoing players included:**
Len Duns, Tommy McLain, R Robinson.

**Sunderland's league record read:**

| P | W | D | L | F | A | Pts | Position |
|---|---|---|---|---|---|-----|----------|
| 42 | 15 | 13 | 14 | 68 | 82 | 43 | 9th |

League appearances (with F.A. Cup appearances in brackets): Aitken 35 (3), Anderson 9 (1), Bingham 19 (2), Davis 11 (1), Fairley 2, Ford 31 (2), Hall 28 (3), Hedley 28 (2), Hudgell 20 (3), Kemp 1, Kirtley 29 (3), Mapson 5, Marston 2, McSeveney 6 (1), Reynolds 22, Shackleton 31 (3), Smith 4, Snell 2, Stelling 34 (1), Threadgold 35 (3), Toseland 6, Walsh 9, Watson 25 (1), Wright (A) 33 (2), Wright (T) 35 (2).

Average home attendance: 40,559.

*Local player Harry Kirtley joined the club in 1948 and spent seven seasons at Roker Park.*

*Argus' opinions about the 1952-1953 season were that "the opportunities of the season were entirely wasted upon an indecisive board and management." Argus continued, "Sunderland started the season without the minimum requirements of a top class full back, a centre half and an outside left and the season ended without any of those positions being filled. Since the decline in the team's performances started in mid December, other weaknesses were recognised but no firm action was taken and the snowball of decline was allowed to reduce the club to one of the most moderate combinations in the league. In the second half of the season when the disapproval of supporters began to sting, scouting missions were increased and a surprising number of them involved players with well established reputations. All met with negative results. One certain fact is that if the second half programme had been tackled from the same precarious position as in the past two seasons, relegation would have been Sunderland's lot this year and nothing would have saved them. The trial and experiment over the entire season has failed to produce solutions to any of the several outstanding problems."*

With Aitken, Ford and T. Wright away on international duty, Sunderland had to make six positional changes for their visit to Ayresome Park. Conditions were ideal for good football. After a good move involving Kirtley and Bingham broke down for Sunderland, a Mannion centre looked troublesome when the ball ran to Delapenha but he was denied a clear view of goal and Kirtley eventually cleared the ball. Shortly afterwards there was a hectic scramble in front of the Sunderland goal when Delapenha took a free kick and McCrae found himself four yards out in front of an open goal. His shot struck Sunderland's Hall and when Stelling raced in to clear, Middlesbrough's best chance of the half had gone. As the first half progressed Sunderland came more and more into the game although they were weak in defence down the left flank but Middlesbrough appeared incapable of cashing in. The best scoring effort of the first half came when a beautifully judged header by Davis was pulled down from under the bar by Ugolini and then Bingham took the ball into the penalty area only to shoot over the bar.

Sunderland started the second half brightly and almost scored in the first few seconds. Stelling headed to Watson who found Kirtley who pushed the ball inside to Bingham who took it on the run to shoot just over the bar. Sunderland took the lead after 72 miutes when Kirtley brilliantly beat Gordon on the half way line before pushing the ball to Bingham who had a long clear run for goal. When he shot from just outside the penalty area, the ball struck a Middlesbrough defender and Davis pounced to shoot past Ugolini. Three minutes later, Middlesbrough were level when a centre from Spuhier was met three yards from goal by McCrae who scored easily. Four minutes from the time Kirtley scored a great goal through a crowded goalmouth to take both points for Sunderland.

**Middlesbrough:** Ugolini, Robinson, Corbett, Bell, Blenkinsopp, Gordon, Mannion, McCrea, Delapenha, Spuhier, Fitzsimons.

**Sunderland:** Threadgold, Stelling, Hudgell, Watson, Hall, Snell, Kirtley, Shackleton, Bingham, Davis, Reynolds.

# 1953-1954

It was prior to the start of the 1953-1954 season that Sunderland were first dubbed "The Bank Of England Club" following close season transfer activity that saw the arrival of goalkeeper Jimmy Cowan from Morton, centre half Ray Daniel from Arsenal and outside left Billy Elliott from Burnley. The total expenditure involved in bringing these three international players to Roker Park was £70,000 and it was a sum which provoked much hostility from other clubs.

Under club chairman Bill Ditchburn, Sunderland became one of the biggest spenders in the game although of his first three major signings only Billy Elliott was an immediate success. Ray Daniel played in the first eleven games of the season before drifting in and out of the side and it was not until the following season that he established himself as regular first choice centre half. Jimmy Cowan did not settle and played his last first team game for the club on 3rd April 1954.

That season, Sunderland conceded eighty nine league goals which was a club record at the time. Sunderland also suffered the indignity of a quick F.A. Cup exit at the hands of Second Divison Doncaster Rovers in a third round tie at Roker Park.

**Incoming players included:**
Ken Chisholm, Jimmy Cowan, Ray Daniel, Billy Elliott, Willie Fraser, K. Jones, Joe McDonald, Ted Purdon, Derek Weddle.

**Outgoing players included:**
Dave Agnew, Trevor Ford, Harry Threadgold, W. Walsh.

**Sunderland's league record read:**

| P | W | D | L | F | A | Pts | Position |
|----|----|----|----|----|----|-----|----------|
| 42 | 14 | 8 | 20 | 81 | 89 | 36 | 18th |

League appearances (with F.A. Cup appearances in brackets): Aitken 34 (1), Anderson 34 (1), Bingham 19 (1), Chisholm 17, Cowan 28 (1), Daniel 27 (1), Davis 3, Elliott 37 (1), Ford 12, Fraser 7, Hall 15, Hedley 29 (1), Hudgell 30 (1), Kemp 1, Kirtley 13 (1), McDonald 3, McNeil 7, McSeveney 6, Purdon 16, Shackleton 38 (1), Sheppeard 1, Snell 4, Stelling 17, Watson 6, Wright (A) 20, Wright (T) 38 (1).

Average home attendance: 43,057.

*Northern Ireland international Billy Bingham spent eight seasons at Sunderland during which time he scored 47 goals in 227 appearances for the club. He left Sunderland for Luton Town in 1958.*

*Argus summed up the events of the 1953-1954 season when he wrote in the Sunderland Football Echo, "Looking back on a season through the eyes of a club which has escaped relegation by only a narrow margin, one finds relief rounding off all the sharp edges of disappointment and dimming the recollection of anxiety and despair. Yet having survived the consequences of the most disastrous run in the club's history, it is of the greatest importance that an accurate picture of events should be carried forward into the close season when the problems surrounding next season's campaign will be considered. It would be wrong and costly to forget the glaring faults and the not so evident ones which have led the side through a chain of poor performances right down to the stage where football had to be forgotten and everything staked upon an all out effort to fight through to safety. Team spirit was never very high at any stage of the season, even in those last few crucial games. To see heated arguments between players of the same side while play is in progress is distressing to say the least. The answer to the problem is discipline and everyone connected with the club must discipline himself to play his own part and to assist everyone to do theirs as well."*

# 1954-1955

The 1954-1955 season was Sunderland's most successful since the resumption of league and F.A. Cup football in 1946.

Manager Bill Murray fielded a more settled side than at any time in the previous eight seasons and the results spoke for themselves.

Sunderland finished the season in fourth position with only goal average separating them from third placed Portsmouth and second placed Wolverhampton and just four points behind the season's champions, Chelsea. That season, Sunderland boasted the second best defensive record, being bettered only by tenth placed Burnley.

The season also saw some full blooded performances in the F.A. Cup. The third round paired Sunderland against Burnley at Roker Park where a crowd of 50,018 saw Billy Elliott score the only goal of the game to set up an away tie at Deepdale where the lads forced a 3-3 draw with goals from Shackleton, Purdon and Chisholm. Sunderland defeated Preston North End in the replay thanks to two Ken Chisholm goals in front of 57,432 supporters on a cold February night. Goals from Fleming and Chisholm at the Vetch Field in the fifth round brought Swansea Town to Roker Park for a replay on 23rd February. Fleming scored the only goal of the game to propel Sunderland into the quarter finals of the F.A. Cup for the first time since 1937.

Sunderland's battling performances in the F.A. Cup were rewarded with a home tie against First Division champions Wolverhampton who were going for the league and cup 'double'. A crowd of almost fifty five thousand made their way to Roker Park for the game which Sunderland won thanks to two goals from Ted Purdon. With the twin towers of Wembley in sight, a mass exodus of supporters made their way to Villa Park for the semi final against Manchester City. Even before the kick off, many observers commented that the pitch was so waterlogged that the game should not go ahead. However, go ahead it did with Manchester City running out 1-0 victors for a place in the F.A. Cup final against Newcastle United.

**Incoming players included:**
Charlie Fleming, Alan O'Neill, Graham Reed.

**Outgoing players included:**
Dickie Davis, Johnny Mapson, Ted McNeill, Thomas Reynolds, Ken Smith, Willie Watson, Arthur Wright, Tommy Wright.

**Sunderland's league record read:**

| P | W | D | L | F | A | Pts | Position |
|---|---|---|---|---|---|-----|----------|
| 42 | 15 | 18 | 9 | 64 | 54 | 48 | 4th |

League appearances (with F.A. Cup appearances in brackets): Aitken 36 (7), Anderson 41 (7), Bingham 35 (7), Bone 2, Chisholm 37 (6), Daniel 38 (7), Dodds 4, Elliott 40 (7), Evans 1, Fleming 13 (4), Fraser 38 (7), Hall 2, Hedley 42 (7), Hudgell 1, Kemp 3, Kirtley 5, McDonald 41 (7), McSeveney 3, Morrison 1, Purdon 36 (5), Shackleton 32 (6), Snell 3, Wood 1, Wright (A) 2, Wright (T) 5.

Average home attendance: 44,226.

*Ken Chisholm graced the Sunderland forward line for just 86 games but during that time he scored 37 goals.*

*Amazingly, the Sunderland Football Echo's Argus was in a most critical mood in his end of season summary when he wrote, "Record books will show that the 1954-1955 season was the most successful in a long lean spell lasting almost twenty years. Running through the events of the season, it is easy to arrive at the conclusion that a good deal more could have been done to bring the side nearer to outright success in pursuing the major honours. Failure to recognise the fact that the attack was not going to make the grade as a combination is the popular charge labelled at those who guide the club's affairs. An attack which could not score its full quota of goals continued its sharp downward trend in the second half of the season and the big prizes slipped out of reach. There are those who set their targets very little higher than the defence of the club's cherished record of never having played in other than the First Division. Those who feel that the club's aim must never be less than the highest honours of the game with due emphasis on team building at all times rather than at times of crises are not pleased with the season's events."*

# 1955-1956

Many supporters will look back on this season as the beginning of a serious decline in Sunderland's fortunes.

The season started promisingly enough with the first dozen games producing nine victories including triumphs over Aston Villa (5-1), Huddersfield Town (3 0) and Arsenal (3-1) at Roker Park and away wins at Aston Villa (4-1), Bolton Wanderers (3-0) and Tottenham Hotspur (3-2).

Although Sunderland's league form was soon to set the alarm bells ringing, there were some dazzling performances in the FA. Cup where the club once again reached the semi-finals of the competition. A hat trick by Fleming put Sunderland on course to beat Norwich City at Roker Park in a third round tie although it took replays at Roker to dispose of York City and Sheffield United in the fourth and fifth rounds respectively. Two goals from new signing Bill Holden were enough to sink Newcastle United at St James Park in front of a crowd of over sixty one thousand. The victory set up a second consecutive semi final appearance, this time against Birmingham City at Hillsborough. However, like the previous season, Sunderland failed to progress to the final as Birmingham City ran out convincing 3-0 winners.

One of the highlights of the season was the visit of Moscow Dynamo to Roker Park on 14th November 1955. The Russian club were the most famous football team in the world at the time and an all ticket crowd of 55,000 flocked to Roker to see the game which Moscow Dynamo won 1-0.

Five days after the visit of Moscow Dynamo, Sunderland set off for Kenilworth Road where Luton Town tore them apart, winning the game 8-2. Although that was the team's heaviest defeat all season, a disastrous second half of the season brought resounding defeats at the hands of Huddersfield Town (4-0), Newcastle United (6-1 and 3-1 defeats on 26th and 27th December), Burnley (4-0) and Manchester City (3-0).

**Incoming players included:**
Johnny Bollands, Alan Graham, Johnny Hannigan, Bill Holden, Jack Maltby.

**Outgoing players included:**
Jimmy Cowan, Fred Hall, Harry Kirtley, Johnny McSeveney, A E Snell.

**Sunderland's league record read:**

| P | W | D | L | F | A | Pts | Position |
|---|---|---|---|---|---|-----|----------|
| 42 | 17 | 9 | 16 | 80 | 95 | 43 | 9th |

League appearances (with F.A. Cup appearances in brackets): Aitken 40 (7), Anderson 37 (7), Bingham 26 (6), Bollands 1, Bolton 2, Bone 7, Chisholm 24 (2), Daniel 34 (7), Dodds 2, Elliott 28 (7), Fleming 36 (7), Fraser 38 (7), Hannigan 7, Hedley 34 (7), Holden 18 (5), Hudgell 3, Kemp 10 (1), McDonald 38 (7), Morrison 4, Purdon 24 (1), Shackleton 28 (6), Stelling 7.

Average home attendance: 37,001.

*Billy Elliott was one of several international players to wear a Sunderland shirt during the fifties.*

*As Sunderland finished the season in a disappointing ninth position, Argus predicted an uneasy close season in which there was so much to be done and so little assurances that it would be done along the right lines. In the Sunderland Football Echo he wrote, "Since the Sunderland recipe for bigger gates and a promise of glory became big spending, it seems that every other aspect of team building has gone overboard. When the crises arrive, as they do with monotonous regularity, it is possible to predict that the club will take one of two courses; spend to the limit or do nothing. The art of carrying out running repairs to a team which is showing weaknesses or building up behind a team which is doing well has been lost entirely. Middle courses could have shaped a more attractive pattern for the future."*

# 1956-1957

An absolutely disastrous season when Sunderland A.F.C. made the headlines for all the wrong reasons.

It promised to be a campaign of mixed fortunes after Sunderland lost their opening game 6-2 at Luton and thrashed Charlton Athletic 8-1 at Roker Park in their fourth game of the season. Sandwiched between these results were a home win (3-0) against Bolton Wanderers and a home defeat (2-1) against Newcastle United.

The season brought an eleven game sequence which yielded just two points. The season's tally of thirty two points was the club's lowest since 1896-1897 season and resulted in the club finishing three points and one place away from relegation. Don Revie signed from Manchester City in November 1956 but because of injury he did not make his Sunderland debut until mid February 1957. It was also a season of woe in the F.A. Cup. Any joy from the 4-0 drubbing of Queens Park Rangers at Roker Park was short lived following a 4-2 defeat at West Bromwich Albion in the fourth round.

Off the field, the club was rocked by allegations of illegal payments being made to certain players. An enquiry by the joint F.A./Football League Commission involved an investigation into the actions of the entire board of directors, manager, accountant and secretary. The findings of the commission sent shock waves through Roker Park as the club was fined £5000 and board members suspended or severely censured while some players were temporarily suspended. The traumas culminated with the resignation of manager Bill Murray on 26th June 1957. One 1st August 1957, Alan Brown arrived as his successor.

*Don Revie signed for Sunderland in November 1956 for a fee of £24,000 from Manchester City. He is seen here with chairman Edward Ditchburn and manager Bill Murray after completing the transfer.*

**Incoming players included:**
Clive Bircham, Harry Clark, Harry Godbold, Johnny Goodchild, Colin Grainger, Jimmy McNab, Don Revie.

**Outgoing players included:**
Ken Chisholm, Bill Holden, Arthur Hudgell, Sam Kemp, Ted Purdon, Derek Weddle.

**Sunderland's league record read:**

| P | W | D | L | F | A | Pts | Position |
|---|---|---|---|---|---|-----|----------|
| 42 | 12 | 8 | 22 | 67 | 88 | 32 | 20th |

League appearances (with F.A. Cup appearances in brackets): Aitken 40 (2), Anderson 36 (2), Bingham 27 (1), Bollands 38 (2), Bolton 1, Bone 2, Chilton 2, Clark 6, Daniel 36 (2), Elliott 36 (2), Fleming 40 (2), Fraser 3, Grainger 13, Hannigan 22 (2), Hedley 42 (2), Hope 9, Hudgell 1, Kemp 2 (1), Maltby 1, McDonald 35 (2), Morrison 13, Purdon 13, Revie 16, Routledge 1, Shackleton 26 (2), Weddle 1.

Average home attendance: 37,531.

*Argus summed up the 1956-1957 season when he wrote at the season's end in the Sunderland Football Echo, "What a tragic season it has been for everyone connected with, or interested in, Sunderland Football Club. Firstly, there was the anxiety of the team's league position which mounted from the early weeks of the season and this was followed by the joint F.A./Football League Commission of enquiry into the club's affairs. Safety from relegation was only assured by the failings of others rather than by the Sunderland team's own efforts. The manner in which the team fought its way into a position from which it finally deserved to stay in the First Division was heartening. By taking eleven points from a possible fourteen in the team's best sequence of the seaon, the Sunderland players brought a little cheer back to the hearts of their success starved supporters. The switching of George Aitken to centre half to work with the new wing half partnership of Don Revie and Billy Elliott was an outstanding success while Jack Hedley was undoubtedly Sunderland's player of the season. However, there are no such grounds for satisfaction in attack. Material from which to build a worthy First Division line for next season is not readily at hand and promising though some of the younger player are, there are unlikely to be any permanent promotions from the reserves to the first team."*

### 1956-1957 Division 1

## PRESTON NORTH END 6 SUNDERLAND 0

*Johnny Bollands pictured at Roker Park in March 1956 shortly after joining the club from Oldham Athletic at a cost of £2,500. Despite establishing himself as first choice goalkeeper the following season, Willie Fraser re-claimed the goalkeeper's shirt in 1957-1958 season.*

Sunderland were torn to shreds by a brilliant Preston side in the first half. After that, Sunderland were just a shambles.

Sunderland were a goal down in the fifth minute when Daniel was beaten to the ball by Baxter who squared the ball to Thompson. From thirty yards out, Thompson was allowed to move forward and pick his spot from the edge of the penalty area to hit a shot past Bollands' right hand. Fifteen minutes later, Dagger centred the ball for Finney to rise above Bollands to head down into goal. When the Sunderland defence hesitated for an offside decision which was not given, Baxter raced through to cross the ball into the middle where it was met by Taylor to turn it past Bollands. When Baxter hit a long ball through for Thompson, the Preston inside forward beat Daniel on the break to score a simple goal. Finney scored a penalty in the 39th minute to send Sunderland in at the interval 5-0 down.

A badly placed clearance by McDonald allowed Thompson to pull the ball down and hit a powerful shot from 25 yards to make it six for Preston.

**Peston North End:**
Else, Cunningham, Walton, Docherty, Dunn, Evans, Thompson, Baxter, Dagger, Finney, Taylor.

**Sunderland:**
Bollands, Hedley, McDonald, Morrison, Daniel, Aitken, Anderson, Purdon, Hannigan, Fleming, Elliott.

**KNIGHTALLS**
*for Everything Furnishing*
SIMPLE OUT OF INCOME PURCHASING SERVICE
1, 2, 3, 4 BLANDFORD STREET

# Sunderland Football
### and Shipping Echo Gazette EDITION Echo

No. 26,981 (85th YEAR)     SATURDAY, APRIL 26, 1958.     TWOPENCE

# SUNDERLAND GO DOWN

## How the Teams Fared Today

### DIVISION I

Birmingham 0 Leicester C. 1
(Half-time: 0—0)
Burnley ..... 3 Bolton W. . 1
(Half-time: 2—0)
Chelsea ..... 2 Man. U. ... 1
(Half-time: 2—1)
Man. City .. 1 Aston V. ... 2
(Half-time: 1—2)
Newcastle . 1 Leeds U. ... 2
(Half-time: 0—0)
Notts F. .... 0 Everton ... 3
(Half-time: 0—0)
Portsmouth 0 Sunderland 2
(Half-time: 0—0)
Preston NE 3 Arsenal .... 0
(Half-time: 2—0)
Sheffield W. 2 Wolves ... 1
(Half-time: 2—0)
Tottenham . 2 Blackpool .. 1
(Half-time: 2—0)
West Brom. 4 Luton Town 2
(Half-time: 1—2)

| | P | W | D | L | F | A | P |
|---|---|---|---|---|---|---|---|
| Wolverhampton | 42 | 28 | 8 | 6 | 103 | 47 | 64 |
| Preston N.E. | 42 | 26 | 7 | 9 | 100 | 51 | 59 |
| Tottenham | 42 | 21 | 9 | 12 | 93 | 77 | 51 |
| West Brom. | 42 | 18 | 14 | 10 | 92 | 70 | 50 |
| Manchester C. | 42 | 22 | 5 | 15 | 104 | 100 | 49 |
| Burnley | 41 | 20 | 5 | 16 | 77 | 73 | 45 |
| Blackpool | 41 | 19 | 6 | 17 | 80 | 67 | 44 |
| Luton Town | 42 | 19 | 6 | 17 | 69 | 63 | 44 |
| Man. Utd. | 42 | 16 | 11 | 15 | 85 | 75 | 43 |
| Nottm F. | 42 | 15 | 12 | 15 | 83 | 79 | 42 |
| Notts Forest | 41 | 16 | 9 | 16 | 68 | 62 | 41 |
| Arsenal | 42 | 16 | 7 | 19 | 73 | 85 | 39 |
| Birmingham | 42 | 14 | 11 | 17 | 76 | 89 | 39 |
| Aston Villa | 41 | 16 | 6 | 19 | 72 | 85 | 38 |
| Bolton W. | 42 | 14 | 10 | 18 | 65 | 87 | 38 |
| Everton | 42 | 13 | 11 | 18 | 65 | 75 | 37 |
| Leeds U. | 41 | 13 | 11 | 17 | 49 | 60 | 37 |
| Leicester C. | 42 | 14 | 5 | 23 | 91 | 112 | 33 |
| Newcastle U. | 41 | 12 | 8 | 21 | 72 | 78 | 32 |
| Chelsea | 41 | 14 | 8 | 22 | 73 | 88 | 32 |
| Sunderland | 42 | 12 | 6 | 24 | 54 | 97 | 32 |
| Sheffield W. | 42 | 12 | 7 | 23 | 69 | 92 | 31 |

### DIVISION II

Bristol City 1 Swansea .. 2
Cardiff City 3 Fulham ...... 0
Charlton A. 3 Blackburn . 4
Doncaster . 1 Ipswich .... 1
(Half-time: 1—1)
Grimsby T. 3 Bristol R. .. 2
Huddersf'ld 0 Lincoln City 1
Leyton O... 0 Sheffield U. 1
(Half-time: 0—1)
Liverpool .. 1 Barnsley ... 1
Middlesbro' 1 West Ham . 3
(Half-time: 1—3)
Rotherham . 1 Notts Co. .. 1
(Half-time: 1—0)
Stoke City . 2 Derby Co. .. 1
(Half-time: 2—0)

| | P | W | D | L | F | A | P |
|---|---|---|---|---|---|---|---|
| West Ham | 42 | 23 | 11 | 8 | 101 | 54 | 57 |
| Blackburn R. | 42 | 22 | 10 | 10 | 93 | 57 | 56 |
| Charlton A. | 42 | 24 | 7 | 11 | 107 | 69 | 55 |
| Liverpool | 42 | 22 | 10 | 10 | 79 | 54 | 54 |
| Sheffield Utd. | 40 | 19 | 11 | 10 | 73 | 49 | 51 |
| Fulham | 40 | 19 | 11 | 10 | 93 | 57 | 49 |
| Middlesbrough | 42 | 19 | 7 | 16 | 83 | 73 | 45 |
| Ipswich T | 42 | 16 | 12 | 14 | 68 | 69 | 44 |
| Huddersfield | 42 | 14 | 16 | 12 | 63 | 66 | 44 |
| Stoke City | 42 | 18 | 6 | 18 | 75 | 73 | 42 |
| Bristol R. | 42 | 17 | 8 | 17 | 85 | 80 | 42 |
| Leyton O. | 42 | 18 | 5 | 19 | 77 | 79 | 41 |
| Grimsby T. | 42 | 17 | 6 | 19 | 86 | 83 | 40 |
| Barnsley | 42 | 14 | 12 | 16 | 70 | 74 | 40 |
| Cardiff City | 41 | 14 | 9 | 18 | 62 | 74 | 37 |
| Derby County | 42 | 14 | 8 | 20 | 60 | 81 | 36 |
| Bristol City | 42 | 13 | 9 | 20 | 63 | 88 | 35 |
| Rotherham | 41 | 14 | 5 | 22 | 64 | 98 | 33 |
| Swansea Town | 42 | 11 | 9 | 22 | 72 | 99 | 31 |
| Notts County | 42 | 12 | 7 | 23 | 88 | 92 | 31 |
| Lincoln C. | 41 | 10 | 9 | 22 | 52 | 81 | 29 |
| Doncaster Rov. | 42 | 8 | 11 | 23 | 56 | 88 | 27 |

### DIVISION III (N)

Barrow ..... 0 Halifax ..... 3
Bradford ... 3 Workington 0
(Half-time: 0—2)
Bury ......... 2 Crewe A. .. 0
Carlisle U. . 0 Bradford C. 3
(Half-time: 0—2)
Chesterfield 2 Darlington . 0
Hartlepools 2 Mansfield .. 0
(Half-time: 1—0)
Oldham A. . 0 Rochdale .. 0
(Half-time: 0—0)
Scunthorpe 2 Chester .... 1
(Half-time: 1—1)
Southport .. 1 Hull City .. 2
(Half-time: 1—1)
Tranmere .. 2 Gateshead . 1
(Half-time: 1—1)
Wrexham .. 1 Accrington . 0
(Half-time: 0—0)
York City .. 0 Stockport .. 0
(Half-time: 0—0)

| | P | W | D | L | F | A | P |
|---|---|---|---|---|---|---|---|
| Scunthorpe | 44 | 27 | 8 | 9 | 83 | 48 | 62 |
| Accrington | 45 | 25 | 10 | 9 | 83 | 56 | 60 |
| Bury | 45 | 23 | 10 | 13 | 94 | 62 | 56 |
| Bradford C. | 45 | 21 | 14 | 10 | 73 | 49 | 56 |
| Hull City | 46 | 19 | 15 | 12 | 78 | 67 | 53 |
| Mansfield T. | 45 | 21 | 8 | 16 | 97 | 92 | 50 |
| Chesterfield | 45 | 18 | 14 | 13 | 71 | 69 | 50 |
| Halifax T. | 45 | 19 | 11 | 15 | 79 | 68 | 49 |
| Stockport Co. | 46 | 18 | 11 | 17 | 74 | 67 | 47 |
| Rochdale | 45 | 19 | 8 | 18 | 76 | 63 | 46 |
| Tranmere R. | 45 | 17 | 10 | 18 | 80 | 75 | 44 |
| Hartlepools Utd. | 46 | 16 | 12 | 17 | 72 | 74 | 44 |
| Carlisle U. | 45 | 15 | 8 | 20 | 79 | 75 | 44 |
| York City | 45 | 15 | 12 | 17 | 67 | 76 | 42 |
| Gateshead | 45 | 15 | 15 | 15 | 68 | 73 | 45 |
| Barrow | 46 | 13 | 15 | 18 | 66 | 74 | 41 |
| Darlington | 44 | 16 | 7 | 21 | 75 | 85 | 39 |
| Bradford | 46 | 13 | 11 | 22 | 68 | 95 | 37 |
| Chester | 45 | 12 | 13 | 20 | 68 | 90 | 37 |
| Southport | 46 | 11 | 6 | 29 | 52 | 88 | 28 |
| Crewe Alex. | 46 | 8 | 7 | 31 | 47 | 95 | 23 |

### DIVISION III (S)

Bournem'th 1 Swindon T. 1
(Half-time: 0—0)
Brentford .. 4 Port Vale .. 1
(Half-time: 1—0)
Colchester . 1 Plymouth .. 2
(Half-time: 1—0)
Coventry C. 1 Gillingham . 1
(Half-time: 1—1)
Crystal Pal. 1 S'thampton 4
(Half-time: 0—3)
N'thampton 1 Southend U. 3
(Half-time: 1—1)
Norwich C. . 1 Aldershot . 3
(Half-time: 1—1)
Shrewsbury v. Exeter C.
Torquay U. 2 Newport Co. 2
(Half-time: 1—2)
Walsall ..... 4 Millwall .... 0
(Half-time: 3—2)
Watford .... 0 Brighton ... 1
(Half-time: 0—0)

| | P | W | D | L | F | A | P |
|---|---|---|---|---|---|---|---|
| Plymouth A. | 45 | 25 | 8 | 13 | 67 | 48 | 58 |
| Brighton | 44 | 23 | 12 | 9 | 82 | 63 | 58 |
| Swindon T. | 45 | 21 | 15 | 9 | 79 | 50 | 57 |
| Brentford | 45 | 23 | 10 | 12 | 81 | 56 | 56 |
| Reading | 46 | 21 | 13 | 12 | 79 | 51 | 55 |
| Southampton | 45 | 20 | 13 | 13 | 110 | 68 | 54 |
| Norwich City | 46 | 19 | 13 | 12 | 75 | 70 | 53 |
| Southend Utd. | 46 | 20 | 11 | 13 | 82 | 53 | 51 |
| Bournemouth | 46 | 20 | 6 | 18 | 72 | 49 | 49 |
| Newport Co. | 46 | 17 | 14 | 15 | 73 | 67 | 48 |
| Queen's P.R. | 45 | 17 | 14 | 14 | 61 | 65 | 48 |
| Colchester U. | 45 | 16 | 13 | 16 | 73 | 77 | 45 |
| Northampton | 45 | 19 | 6 | 20 | 84 | 73 | 44 |
| Crystal Palace | 45 | 13 | 18 | 10 | 70 | 72 | 43 |
| Watford | 45 | 12 | 14 | 16 | 59 | 71 | 42 |
| Port Vale | 45 | 16 | 10 | 19 | 66 | 55 | 42 |
| Aldershot | 46 | 12 | 16 | 18 | 59 | 89 | 40 |
| Coventry | 45 | 13 | 13 | 19 | 59 | 78 | 39 |
| *Shrewsbury | 44 | 14 | 10 | 20 | 48 | 68 | 38 |
| Walsall | 45 | 14 | 9 | 23 | 61 | 69 | 37 |
| Gillingham | 45 | 12 | 9 | 24 | 49 | 78 | 33 |
| *Exeter City | 45 | 11 | 9 | 25 | 57 | 98 | 31 |
| Millwall | 46 | 11 | 9 | 26 | 63 | 91 | 31 |

* Late kickoff

### Amateur International

England ...... 1 France ... 1
(Half-time: 1—1)

### Highest Score
**EAST STIRLINGSHIRE 5 RANGERS 5**

### Highest Aggregate
**Charlton 3, Blackburn 4**

### Scottish Cup: Final
Clyde .... 1 Hibernian .. 0
(Half-time: 1—0)

### Scottish League (A)
Dundee .... 1 Airdrie ..... 3
(Half-time: 0—1)
Kilmarnock 1 Raith R. .... 1
(Half-time: 0—0)
Motherwell 1 Th'd L'nark 2
(Half-time: 0—0)
Queen of S. 2 St Mirren .. 2
(Half-time: 0—0)
Rangers .... 5 Aberdeen .. 2
(Half-time: 3—0)

### UPS AND DOWNS

**DIVISION I**
Champions—Wolverhampton Wands.; runners-up, Preston N.E.
Relegated — Sheffield W. and Sunderland.

**DIVISION II**
Promoted — West Ham, Blackburn.
Relegated — Doncaster R.

**LEAGUE III (NORTH)**
Promoted — Scunthorpe U.

## HOMES

| | |
|---|---|
| STENH'SEMUIR | BURY |
| RANGERS | TOTTENHAM H |
| COWDENBEATH | WEST BROM A |
| E. STIRLING | ST JOHNSTONE |
| CLYDE | CARDIFF C |
| MONTROSE | BRENTFORD |
| HARTLEPOOLS | SCUNTHORPE |
| SHEFFIELD W | CHESTERFIELD |
| PRESTON N.E. | WREXHAM |
| WALSALL | STOKE CITY |
| CHELSEA | GRIMSBY T. |
| BURNLEY | TRANMERE R. |

## AWAYS

| | |
|---|---|
| SOUTHEND U. | ALDERSHOT |
| LINCOLN C | BRIGHTON |
| ASTON VILLA | SUNDERLAND |
| SWANSEA T. | AIRDRIE |
| PLYMOUTH A | DUNDEE UTD. |
| WEST HAM U. | LEICESTER |
| HULL CITY | BLACKBURN R. |
| LEEDS UTD. | BRADFORD C. |
| EVERTON | HALIFAX T. |
| ARBROATH | SOUTHAMPTON |
| NOTTS CO. | SHEFFIELD U. |

## DRAWS
YORK CITY v STOCKPORT
OLDHAM v ROCHDALE
BRADFORD v WORKINGTON
BOURNEMOUTH v SWINDON
QU'EN OF SOUTH v ST MIRREN
MORTON v DUNFERMLINE
KILMARNOCK v RAITH ROV.
COVENTRY v GILLINGHAM
DONCASTER v IPSWICH T.
LIVERPOOL v BARNSLEY
TORQUAY v NEWPORT

### NORTH-EASTERN LEAGUE
Darl'gt'n R. 2 Spennymoor 1
Stockton .. 2 Carlisle R. . 5
Sund. R. ... 4 Horden ..... 0
W. Stanley 0 Consett ..... 2

---

## Victory at Pompey Was Too Little and Too Late!

## LEICESTER ALSO WIN

**Sunderland today lost their distinction of never having played in any but the First Division. In spite of a last-ditch victory, they are relegated for the first time in 68 years. Leicester City also won.**

### PORTSMOUTH — 0    SUNDERLAND — 2

RAIN fell steadily an hour or two before the start of Sunderland's vital League game against Portsmouth at Fratton Park this afternoon. Because the ground was firm this morning, however, it meant that only the surface itself would be soft.

Portsmouth expected quite a big attendance but the rain may have kept many would-be spectators away. The covered accommodation was popular enough but there were huge gaps in the uncovered portions of the ground which meant that there were little more than 15,000 present at the start.

Sunderland turned out as selected but Portsmouth had to make a late change after Dougan had failed to pass a fitness test. The centre forward position was taken over by Crawford.

**PORTSMOUTH**
Uprichard
McGhee    Gunter
Dickinson   Rutter   Carter
Gordon   Crawford   Bernard
Harris      Crawford      Govan

Grainger   Kichenbrand   Fogarty
O'Neill         Revie
Pearce   Hurley   Anderson
Elliott   Hedley
Fraser
**SUNDERLAND**

Referee: Mr R. J. Leafe, of Nottingham.

Revie won the toss and Sunderland took advantage of the cross-wind. A well-timed tackle by Elliott checked a Pompey move down the left and when Kichenbrand got back to lend a hand the ball was driven down the middle

### By ARGUS

where O'Neill tried unsuccessfully to move ahead of McGhee and Rutter. Anderson, Revie and O'Neill combined well in midfield but the wing half's pass down the wing was out of play before Fogarty could reach it.

Players of both sides were having difficulty in getting a foothold on the treacherous surface.

Revie was in trouble near the corner flag when challenged by Gunter. He managed to get the ball over at the second attempt but there was no Sunderland player near enough to make contact with him.

### Two Chances

Grainger handled the ball in bringing it under control when moving inside and from the resulting free kick Portsmouth built up an attack which gave them two chances of going ahead. The first came when the ball was lobbed over Hurley's head and Crawford
Continued in Back Page

**LATEST**

*Sixty eight years of continuous First Division membership ended for Sunderland on 26th April, 1958.*

# 1957-1958

For the first time in post war years, Sunderland kicked off the new season with a new manager. Alan Brown was a disciplinarian with definite ideas about the game and it came as no surprise when he made sweeping changes to the playing personnel. Alan Brown was a fitness fanatic and his approach to training was not universally well received. Club captain Don Revie was quoted as saying that pre season training was the most vigorous he had known while Len Shackleton retired after the first game of the season.

The first eleven games produced just three victories while twenty two goals were conceded. Following this sequence of results, Alan Brown made his first signing when he paid £18,000 to Millwall for Charlie Hurley's signature. The introduction of a new centre half to the team did not immediately have the desired result as the first two games with Hurley in the team resulted in heavy defeats at Blackpool (7-0) and Burnley (6-0). Further heavy defeats at Aston Villa (5-2) and Luton Town (7-1) as well as a 6-1 hammering by Birmingham City at Roker Park meant that Sunderland were definite relegation candidates long before the end of the season.

The ninety seven goals conceded in the 1957-1958 season was the worst defensive record in the club's history and one which saw the club relegated for the first time, thus bringing to an end sixty eight years of First Division membership.

The F.A. Cup failed to produce a single crumb of comfort; Sunderland losing at Goodison Park in a third round replay against Everton.

**Incoming players included:**
Len Ashurst, Ambrose Fogarty, Martin Harvey, Charlie Hurley, Don Kichenbrand, Ian Lawther, Reg Pearce, Dickie Rooks, Alan Spence, George Whitelaw.

**Outgoing players included:**
Laurie Bolton, Ray Daniel, Len Shackleton.

**Sunderland's league record read:**

| P | W | D | L | F | A | Pts | Position |
|---|---|---|---|---|---|-----|----------|
| 42 | 10 | 12 | 20 | 54 | 97 | 32 | 21st |

League appearances (with F.A. Cup appearances in brackets): Aitken 32, Anderson 39 (2), Bingham 30 (2), Chilton 1, Elliott 42 (2), Fleming 15 (2), Fogarty 24 (2), Fraser 33 (2), Godbold 5 (1), Goodchild 7, Graham 3, Grainger 30 (1), Hannigan 4, Hedley 35, Hurley 22 (2), Kichenbrand 10, Maltby 6, McDonald 19 (2), O'Neill 32, Pearce 12, Reed 5 (2), Revie 39 (2), Routledge 1, Shackleton 1, Spence 5, Whitelaw 2.

*One of manager Alan Brown's first signings was half back Reg Pearce who joined the club from Luton Town for £16,000 in February 1958.*

Average home attendance: 36,070.

*Despite the fact that Sunderland had just surrendered their proud record of never having played outside the First Division, the end of season summary by Argus was less harsh than might have been expected, he wrote, "Sunderland lost their distinction of never having played in any but the First Division. In spite of a last ditch victory at Portsmouth today, Sunderland are relegated for the first time in sixty eight years. Now that one of the most depressing seasons in the club's history is behind them, Sunderland must get on with planning for the future; it is the way ahead that counts now. The side which finished the season at Fratton Park is simply not a proposition for a team next season. Over the last few weeks it has been possible to descern a steady rise in the team's tactical approach to the game, even though it has not been sufficiently marked to achieve the desired trend in results. The team has been playing or attempting to play, to an overall pattern which is based upon fundamentals and is designed in time, to produce a distinctive team style. The club's fortunes have suffered a shattering blow during the teething period of the new system. The anticipated sharp rise to a high level of performance may still be some way ahead but we are one season nearer to production date."*

| 1957-1958 Division 1 | PORTSMOUTH 0    SUNDERLAND 2 |
|---|---|

Rain fell steadily for two hours before Sunderland's vital league game at Fratton Park. Revie won the toss and Sunderland took advantage of the cross wind. Both sets of players struggled to cope with the treacherous surface. Sunderland conceded an early free kick when Grainger handled the ball and Sunderland were fortunate to survive when the ball was lobbed over Hurley's head only for Crawford to shoot straight at Fraser. Sunderland had their share of possession but needed Hurley to be at his best as the defence came under increasing pressure. Sunderland took the lead in the 41st minute when Pearce put Kichenbrand through. The centre forward neatly moved inside Gunter before crashing home an unstoppable shot from ten yards.

Sunderland almost increased their lead at the start of the second half when O'Neill was unlucky to see his goalbound shot beaten down. As the Rokermen pressed forward in search of a second goal they were lucky not to concede an equaliser when Elliott cleared on the line with Fraser beaten. Fraser then brought off a magnificent save from Gordon before Kichenbrand scored his and Sunderland's second goal when he lobbed the ball over the advancing goalkeeper in the 89th minute.

Despite this last ditch victory, Sunderland were relegated for the first time in their history as fellow strugglers Leicester City also won their game.

**Portsmouth:** Uprichard, McGhee, Gunter, Dickinson, Rutter, Carter, Gordon, Bernard, Harris, Crawford, Govan.

**Sunderland:** Fraser, Hedley, Elliott, Anderson, Hurley, Pearce, Revie, O'Neill, Fogarty, Kichenbrand, Grainger.

# 1958-1959

Sunderland's start to their first season in the Second Division could hardly have been worse. Off the field, captain Don Revie shocked the club by asking for a transfer while the first game at Lincoln City produced and emphatic 3-1 defeat, followed by a 2-1 reversal against Fulham at Roker Park. A shocking run of defeats during September against Swansea Town (5-0), Sheffield Wednesday (6-0), Ipswich Town (2-0) and Bristol Rovers (2-1) contributed towards Sunderland's bottom placing in the Second Division with just eight points from the first fourteen games.

Despite a third round F.A. Cup exit against Everton for the second year running, Sunderland's league form gradually improved to the extent that they finished the season in a position of mid table respectability.

**Incoming players included:** John Fraser, Cecil Irwin, Colin Nelson, Jimmy O'Neill, Dominick Sharkey, Ernie Taylor, Peter Wakeham.

**Outgoing players included:**
George Aitken, Billy Bingham, John Bone, Harry Clark, Charlie Fleming, Willie Fraser, Alan Graham, Johnny Hannigan, Joe McDonald, William Morrison, Don Revie, Jack Stelling, George Whitelaw.

**Sunderland's league record read:**

| P | W | D | L | F | A | Pts | Position |
|---|---|---|---|---|---|-----|----------|
| 42 | 16 | 8 | 18 | 64 | 75 | 40 | 15th |

League appearances (with F.A. Cup appearances in brackets): Aitken 4, Anderson 41 (1), Ashurst 33 (1), Bircham 26, Bollands 6, Elliott 9, Fogarty 3, Fraser (J) 9, Fraser (W) 9, Godbold 6, Goodchild 27 (1), Grainger 36 (1), Hedley 12, Hurley 35 (1), Irwin 1, Kichenbrand 40 (1), Maltby 7 (1), McNab 10, Nelson 29 (1), O'Neill 12, Pearce 42 (1), Revie 9, Robson 3, Taylor 22 (1), Wakeham 28 (1), Whitelaw 3.

Average home attendance: 27,773

*Don Kichenbrand in action during his best season in a Sunderland shirt, 1958-1959, in which he scored 21 goals in 40 appearances.*

*At the end of Sunderland's first ever season in the Second Division, Argus wrote in the Sunderland Football Echo, "It has been a tough season, worrying in many respects and one which, outwardly at least, gives very little cause of satisfaction. Throughout the season Sunderland have had to search for a starting point towards team building and the first essential was that the atmosphere should be right for such a project. Though success in this direction is not evident in any tangible form, I can tell you that Sunderland are now together as a team with just the right atmosphere to tackle the big job which lies ahead. It is satisfying to realise that this was achieved while the relegation threat was at its height and that the new spirit which sprang from it carried the side to safety. From a playing point of view, the position reached in the reorganisation of the side is no more than a starting point. Of the team on duty in the closing game of the season, only Stan Anderson and Colin Grainger were on the club's books at the beginning of last season. Since then, nineteen players have made their debut in Sunderland's colours and nine of them have managed to hold their places. I believe there is the assurance of better entertainment next season when supporters will be entitled to look for improvement. If Sunderland can manage to force the pace, even at substantial cost, I think they will reap a very rich reward."*

# 1959-1960

Following the shakey baptism to Second Division football in 1958-1959 season, most supporters hoped for better times in the new campaign. However, it was not to be and Sunderland had slipped one place lower in the Second Division after being trounced 3-0 at Liverpool in the final game of the season. Sixteenth position in the Second Division was thus Sunderland's lowest ever end of season ranking and chairman Stanley Ritson commented that he had noticed a state of hysteria in the town as relegation to the Third Division had at one time seemed to be a distinct possibility.

Although the team's results did not reflect the fact, Sunderland's performances were improving and a stable side was beginning to emerge from the team rebuilding programme. The half back line of Anderson/Hurley/McNab was already established and the general feeling was that the main element lacking in the team was experience.

Manager Alan Brown announced his retained list on 30th April 1960 and a significant feature of the list of 34 players was that the average age was just over 20 years. The list was as follows:-

Retained: Anderson, Ashurst, Borne, Crudace, Davison, Dillon, Fogarty, Godbold, Goodchild, Grainger, Harvey, Hird, Hurley, Irwin, Jones, Kiernan, Lackenby, Lawther, Lewis, Maltby, McNab, McPheat, Nelson, O'Neill A., O'Neill J., Ord, Peace, Potter, Rooks, Smith, Taylor, Topley, Wakeham and Wardle.

Transfer List: Fraser, Kichenbrand, Robson and Spence.

Free Transfers: Buchanan, Carrick, Clark, Dodds, Grieveson, Ingham, Ramshaw, Richardson J., Rodden, Turner, Wilson, Wood and Young.

Sunderland made what was by now their traditional exit from the F.A. Cup at the third round stage, this time at the hands of Blackburn Rovers when they lost the replay 4-1 at Ewood Park.

**Incoming players included:**
Jimmy Davison, John Dillon, Willie McPheat.

**Outgoing players included:**
Clive Bircham, Johnny Bollands, Fred Chilton, Billy Elliott, Jack Hedley, Graham Reed.

**Sunderland's league record read:**

| P | W | D | L | F | A | Pts | Position |
|---|---|---|---|---|---|-----|----------|
| 42 | 12 | 12 | 18 | 52 | 65 | 36 | 16th |

League appearances (with F.A. Cup appearances in brackets): Anderson 41 (2), Ashurst 32 (2), Bircham 2, Bollands 7, Davison 9, Fraser 12, Fogarty 37 (2), Godbold 1, Goodchild 9, Grainger 41 (2), Harvey 5, Hurley 38 (2), Irwin 7, Jones 10, Kichenbrand 3, Lawther 38 (2), Maltby 5, McNab 36 (2), Nelson 35 (2), O'Neill 14 (2), Pearce 6, Robson 2, Sharkey 1, Taylor 36 (2), Wakeham 35 (2).

Average home attendance: 23,344.

*Stan Anderson was a first team player at Roker Park for twelve seasons. His 447 games for the club are exceeded only by Len Ashurst (452), John Doig (456) and Jimmy Montgomery (623).*

*In one of his most straight talking summaries of the concluding season, Argus echoed the views of the majority of Sunderland supporters when he wrote, "Two anxious seasons in the Second Division do not appear to have made the slightest difference to the board's attitude towards the need for a change in policy. Far from building up from the promotion bid which supporters are entitled to expect from a club of Sunderland's stature, the means have not even been forthcoming to provide safeguards against the threat of further relegation. In the two bitter years since First Division status was surrendered, the purse strings have been relaxed for the payment of only three minor fees for players. What a sad commentary upon the state of affairs within a club which has been one of the best supported in the land. Little wonder that this lack of positive action has led to the spread of apathy among supporters. And though by Roker Park standards the drop to an average home gate for league matches of less than 23,000 is akin to catastrophe, the board can thank their lucky stars that there were so many loyal supporters prepared to share their hope for the future."*

# 1960-1961

Sunderland finally emerged as a team with genuine promotional credentials and, but for two indifferent spells at either end of the season, they would have been serious contenders for championship honours. For the first time since relegation they won the opening game of the season; a 2-1 victory against Swansea Town at Roker Park but they suffered five consecutive defeats. A topsy turvy season then produced a run of just one defeat in twenty games and with it came real hope that the team would stage a late promotion push. However, five defeats in the final ten games of the season put paid to all hopes of a return to the First Division.

After the recent quick exits from the F.A. Cup, the 1960-1961 season at last gave Sunderland fans something to shout about. A fine 2-1 home victory over Arsenal set Sunderland up for a trip to Anfield where Liverpool were themselves beginning to emerge as promotion hopefuls. Goals from Hooper and Lawther, without reply from the Merseysiders put Sunderland into the fifth round draw which paired them with Norwich City and a difficult away trip to Carrow Road. A mass exodus from Wearside meant that 42,000 fans packed into the Norfolk ground to see Charlie Hurley score the only goal of the game and send Sunderland through to the quarter finals of the competition for the first time in five years. The home tie against Tottenham Hotspur was, potentially, Sunderland's most difficult game since leaving the First Division. Tottenham Hotspur were runaway leaders at the time and eventually won the First Division championship with a post war scoring record of one hundred and fifteen league goals. Tottenham's Cliff Jones gave the Londoners a first half lead although Willie McPheat equalised early in the second half to create one of the most deafening Roker Roars ever heard. Roker Park was bursting at the seams that day with 61,236 supporters packed into the ground and with a panic stricken Spurs defence struggling to cope with the Sunderland onslaught, a 1-1 draw was something of an anticlimax. This had undoubtedly been Sunderland's best chance to win the tie as the replay at White Hart Lane was more in line with the form book, Tottenham running out convincing 5-0 winners on their way to the ultimate League and F.A. Cup double.

The Football League Cup was introduced for the first time during the 1960-1961 season although most of the bigger clubs declined to enter. Sunderland did enter and were drawn away to Brentford in the first round on 25th October 1961. Despite storming into a 3-1 lead with goals from Fogarty, Lawther and McPheat, Sunderland lost the game 4-3 to their Third Division opponents.

Notable first team debutants included Martin Harvey, Harry Hooper and Jimmy Montgomery.

**Incoming players included:**
George Herd, Keith Hird, Harry Hopper, Tommy Mitchinson, Jimmy Montgomery, Jack Overfield, Brian Usher.

**Outgoing players included:**
Leslie Dodds, John Fraser, Harry Godbold, Colin Grainger, K. Jones, Don Kichenbrand, Alan O'Neill, Reg Pearce, Alan Spence, Ernie Taylor.

**Sunderland's league record read:**

| P | W | D | L | F | A | Pts | Position |
|---|---|---|---|---|---|---|---|
| 42 | 17 | 13 | 12 | 75 | 60 | 47 | 6th |

*Ian Lawther, Peter Wakeham and Charlie Hurley pose for the camera during a training session at Roker Park in 1960. All three players were brought to the club by Alan Brown.*

League appearances (with F.A. Cup and League Cup appearances in brackets): Anderson 41 (6), Ashurst 40 (6), Davison 11, Dillon 17 (5), Fogarty 41 (6), Goodchild 1, Harvey 5 (1), Herd 1, Hird 1, Hooper 26 (6), Hurley 35 (6), Irwin 11, Lawther 37 (6), Maltby 3, McNab 40 (5), McPheat 26 (6), Nelson 42 (6), O'Neill 7, Overfield 23 (1), Pearce 1, Rooks 5, Sharkey 4, Taylor 10, Wakeham 41 (6).

Average home attendance: 28,995.

*Despite the fact that Sunderland had progressed to finish the season no higher than sixth position in the Second Division, Argus was in optimistic mood when considering the team's prospects for the season ahead when he wrote, "For me, this has been a very fruitful season indeed... a season in which all the tremendous hard work behind the scenes has brought the promise of success. The exciting prospect of an all-out Sunderland drive for promotion next season becomes brighter still with the end of season signing of Scottish International inside right George Herd. Though it is too early to judge how near the team is to being worthy of the big promotion prize, it is my confident belief that the team which eventually carries them back to the First Division will not vary greatly from the one which closed the current season. The last happy twist was the signing of Herd who is regarded as made to measure for the role of shaping a young attack into the type of scoring machine needed for a promotion drive. An extremely young defence and half back line has won wide acclaim for the part they have played in reviving the club's fortunes while there have been pleasing signs in attack, even though the whole picture is not yet one of outstanding success. However, the upsurge of talent forecast three years ago is on its way in the wake of the big drive at senior level."*

**FA Cup (Sixth Round) 1960-1961**      **SUNDERLAND 1   TOTTENHAM HOTSPUR 1**

Tottenham pushed forward early in the game and when they won a throw-in about 20 yards from the corner flag, MacKay astonished everyone by throwing the ball into the centre of the six yard line which Hurley won in the air, with Fogarty completing the clearance. After nine minutes, Tottenham won a corner and when the kick was forced out to Jones he headed over a bunch of players in front of goal and passed an unsighted Wakeham into the net. Sunderland surged forward with several strong attacks but were unable to score an equaliser. As the game progressed, Tottenham's man to man passing from midfield to attack became a strong feature of the game with Sunderland struggling to find an answer.

The second half started with Sunderland pressing forward strongly and it was no surprise when they equalised after fifty minutes. After a shot was beaten down by the Tottenham goalkeeper, the ball ran along the line and McPheat lead the rush of Sunderland players to the ball to force it into the net. The Roker Roar became deafening as Tottenham defended desperately to keep Sunderland out. Sunderland won three corners in quick succession and even the normally cool headed MacKay was booting the ball anywhere to relieve the intense pressure. As the game drew to a close, Sunderland were unlucky not to take the lead when a shot from Dillon was saved on the line by Brown.

**Sunderland:** Wakeham, Nelson, Ashurst, Anderson, Hurley, McNab, Fogarty, McPheat, Hooper, Lawther, Dillon.

**Tottenham Hotspur:** Brown, Baker, Henry, Blanchflower, Norman, MacKay, White, Allen, Jones, Smith, Oryson.

# 1961-1962

The excited anticipation of what the new season held in store was enhanced by the signing of Middlesbrough free scoring forward Brian Clough. Clough cost Sunderland £39,500 and made an immediate impact during his first season at Sunderland when he scored twenty nine league goals including hat tricks against Bury, Plymouth Argyle, Swansea Town and Huddersfield Town.

Despite some exciting performances and excellent results, it proved to be a case of so near and yet so far as far as promotion was concerned. Sunderland needed a win in their last game of the season at Swansea to guarantee promotion. It was not to be Sunderland's day as Swansea hung on for a 1-1 draw and in doing so condemned Sunderland to another season in the Second Division.

Progress in the F.A. Cup was restricted to a 3-0 victory in a third round replay at Southampton; Sunderland losing a fourth round replay tie at Port Vale. In the League Cup, there were successes against Bolton Wanderers, Walsall and Hull City before Sunderland crashed out 4-1 at home to Norwich City.

**Incoming players included:**
Norman Clarke, Brian Clough.

**Outgoing players included:**
Johnny Goodchild, Ian Lawther, Jack Maltby.

**Sunderland's league record read:**

| P | W | D | L | F | A | Pts | Position |
|---|---|---|---|---|---|-----|----------|
| 42 | 22 | 9 | 11 | 85 | 50 | 53 | 3rd |

League appearances (with F.A. Cup and League Cup appearances in brackets): Anderson 38 (8), Ashurst 42 (9), Clough 34 (9), Davison 9 (2), Dillon 1, Fogarty 24 (3), Harvey 4 (1), Herd 32 (7), Hooper 33 (8), Hurley 33 (9), Irwin 33 (7), Montgomery 11 (1), McNab 42 (9), McPheat 29 (8), Nelson 9 (2), O'Neill 7, Overfield 40 (8), Rooks 9, Sharkey 1, Wakeham 30 (8).
Average home attendance: 32,687.

*Dickie Rooks graduated to Sunderland's first team via Alan Brown's youth policy.*

*Sunderland's brave attempt to win promotion to the First Division in 1961-1962 season faltered at the final hurdle when they failed to win the last game of the season at Swansea. However even before that game Argus continued his support for Alan Brown's style of football management when he wrote, "The final account of the season has still to be written but even at this stage Sunderland players and officials know that the 1961-1962 season's work will be written into the record book with special affection. This was the season which marked Sunderland's first firm steps out of the wilderness of Second Division football each taken with the certainty that the return to the First Division could not be long delayed. It was always the long term forecast that the real surge of power throughout the Sunderland teams would not come until the youth development scheme had had a real impact upon the senior side. The scheme was launched five years ago out of dire necessity because of the club's appalling financial situation. It was always obvious that the youth policy could never be expected to meet all requirements alone and that a wise spending policy would have to go hand in hand with it. Despite the temptation from time to time to gamble on a short term build up, the policy has been carried out faithfully and with extremely satisfying results. It is only a few months since supporters were being asked to believe that the youth scheme had been a failure. The truth is self evident. It has been an unqualified success and now that the first wave has hit the senior team in strength, it is encouraging to look at the second and third waves and see the promising young players being shaped into first team material of future seasons."*

## 1962-1963

The season started well for Sunderland with four wins and a draw from their first six league games with Brian Clough continuing his goal scoring exploits. By the time George Mulhall and Johnny Crossan had been signed from Aberdeen and Standard Leige respectively, the formation of the team had taken on a decidedly settled appearance.

Once again, promotion rested upon the last game of the season and once again Sunderland just missed out. They needed only to draw against Chelsea at Roker Park but in front of 47,955 supporters their bombardment of the Londoners' penalty area failed to produce a goal and a Tommy Harmer effort gave Chelsea the points and promotion ahead of Sunderland on goal average. Thus for the second successive season, Sunderland's promotion effort was thwarted in the final game of the season.

In the F.A. Cup, Sunderland progressed to the fifth round, beating Preston North End and Gravesend before falling to Coventry City at Highfield Road. Meanwhile, encouraging performances in the League Cup allowed Sunderland to go all the way to the quarter final stage before losing out to Aston Villa in a two legged tie.

**Incoming players included:**
Johnny Crossan, Andy Kerr, Joe Kiernan, Gary Moore, George Mulhall.

**Outgoing players included:**
John Dillon, Jimmy O'Neill, Jack Overfield, Peter Wakeham.

**Sunderland's league record read:**

| P | W | D | L | F | A | Pts | Position |
|---|---|---|---|---|---|-----|----------|
| 42 | 20 | 12 | 10 | 84 | 55 | 52 | 3rd |

League appearances (with F.A. Cup and League Cup appearances in brackets): Anderson 35 (7), Ashurst 40 (11), Clarke 4 (1), Clough 24 (4), Crossan 24 (8), Davison 33 (8), Fogarty 20 (9), Harvey 9 (5), Herd 40 (7), Hooper 6 (1), Hurley 38 (10), Irwin 17 (1), Kerr (A) 8, Kiernan 1 (1), McNab 38 (9), McPheat 3, Mitchinson 2, Montgomery 42 (11), Mulhall 35 (10), Nelson 25 (10), Overfield 1, Rooks 4 (1), Sharkey 9 (7).

*Cecil Irwin made his Second Division debut as a sixteen year old in 1958-1959 season.*

Average home attendance: 36,725.

*Argus writing in the Sunderland Football Echo made this end of season comment, "The Sunderland team today are immeasurably stronger in every respect than the Sunderland of twelve months ago. And the power to keep them rising in stature to take their place among the best in the land is still safely in the hands of Alan Brown, the man who weathered the early storms in the face of badly informed criticism and is finally reaping his reward. Sunderland supporters can never thank him enough for the magnificent job of work he has done and will continue to do so to ensure that, step by step, the Sunderland team goes forward to take its place at the top. Points and position in the league are the first indication of how a club stands. But Sunderland's rise is also indicated by the extent to which those supporters who had begun to drift away long before Mr Brown joined the club are now coming back to pledge their votes of confidence. The happy partnership between the club and its supporters has been renewed on the old scale and together they are all set to open the big offensive on a broad front."*

**Division 2 1962-1963**

## SUNDERLAND 0    CHELSEA 1

With fears of overcrowding being widely publicised, the Sunderland Football Echo reported that there were only about 50,000 inside the ground at kick off.

Sunderland won their first corner in the third minute after good work by Davison and Mulhall created an opening for Herd. Shortly afterwards, Mulhall attacked on the left and when he made a backward centre, Herd hit a good shot which brought a brilliant diving save out of Bonetti. Most of the early attacking play came from Sunderland and it was not until 25 minutes that Chelsea won their first corner. Tambling made it an inswinger which kept low and swung towards the rear post where Harmer got the necessary touch to score. Crossan, Sharkey and Mulhall all had chances to equalise but the Chelsea defence — and Bonetti in particular — thwarted their efforts.

With a strong wind behind them in the second half, Sunderland piled on the pressure but it was all to no avail. As Sunderland threw more and more into attack in search of the equaliser which would secure promotion, Bonetti finger tipped a Mulhall drive behind for a corner and then could only watch as a Herd header dropped just over the bar. In the later stages of the second half, play was almost entirely concentrated in the Chelsea half but the goal just would not come and as the Londoners took both points — and promotion — Sunderland could only reflect on what might have been.

**Sunderland:** Montgomery, Nelson, Ashurst, Anderson, Hurley, McNab, Herd, Crossan, Davison, Sharkey, Mulhall.

**Chelsea:** Bonetti, Shellito, McCreadie, Venables, Mortimore, Harris, Kevan, Harmer, Blunstone, Upton, Tambling.

# 1963-1964

Sunderland were promoted in style before the final game of the season. The record books show that Sunderland were beaten only once during the last eighteen games of the season and their magnificent away form produced a haul of twenty six points from a possible forty two and in doing so set a club record. The club suffered only six defeats all season and a measure of the stability of the side was that nine players wore a first team shirt in thirty seven or more league games.

It was also a good season for Sunderland in the F.A. Cup. The club was drawn at home in the third, fourth and fifth rounds against Northampton Town, Bristol City and Everton respectively. Particularly pleasing was the 3-1 defeat of First Division Everton at Roker Park not least of all because it set up a tantalising away tie with mighty Manchester United. The tie turned out to be one of the greatest epics in Sunderland's history. A 3-3 draw at Old Trafford brought Manchester United to Roker Park for the replay. At one stage, Sunderland were leading 3-1 at Old Trafford and it took an 88th minute equaliser from George Best to deny them victory at the first attempt. Sunderland supporters were confidently predicting a home win in the replay and while the official attendance was put at 46,727, a collapsed door at the ground enabled many thousands of people to gain free admittance. Unofficial estimates list the attendance at 70,000 with another 30,000 being locked out. On two occasions Sunderland took the lead against their First Division opponents and again it took an equaliser in the 88th minute — this time from Bobby Charlton — to save Manchester United's skin. This set up a second replay at Huddersfield and although Sunderland once again took the lead, Manchester United eventually ran out 5-1 winners. In the League Cup, it was an early exit for Sunderland, a 3-1 defeat at Swansea Town in the first round.

**Incoming players included:**
Dave Elliott, Jimmy Shoulder, Mel Slack.

**Outgoing players included:**
Stan Anderson, Jimmy Davison, Ambrose Fogarty, Keith Hird, Harry Hooper, Andy Kerr, Joe Kiernan.

**Sunderland's league record read:**

| P | W | D | L | F | A | Pts | Position |
|---|---|---|---|---|---|-----|----------|
| 42 | 25 | 11 | 6 | 81 | 37 | 61 | 2nd |

League appearances (with F.A. Cup and League Cup appearances in brackets): Anderson 10 (1), Ashurst 42 (7), Crossan 42 (7), Elliott 5 (3), Fogarty 3, Harvey 32 (6), Herd 39 (7), Hurley 41 (6), Irwin 39 (7), Kerr (A) 10 (1), McNab 37 (4), Mitchinson 1, Montgomery 42 (7), Mulhall 42 (7), Nelson 3, Rooks (1), Sharkey 33 (6), Usher 41 (7).

*Three Roker stalwarts from the early sixties; Ambrose Fogarty, Jimmy McNab and Len Ashurst.*

# SUNDERLAND WIN THE POINTS AND HIT THE PINK!

## Football Echo Flushes With Success

THE Football Echo, which turned white on April 26, 1958, when for the first time Sunderland Football Club were relegated to Division II, then to blue at the start of the following season, tonight resumes its

### PROMOTION ASSURED

AS a result of today's matches Sunderland are assured of promotion to Division One, having established a lead over Preston North End which cannot be overcome with only one more game to be played. To mark the occasion, the Football Echo turns pink again, and publishes a four-page supplement on the victorious season.

traditional pink colour in celebration of the team's return to the First Division. The "Pink 'Un" first turned white towards the end of the 1912-13 season. The change was made because supplies of pink paper could not be obtained, but the first edition appeared on the nighs of Sunderland's defeat by Aston Villa in the Cup Final at Crystal Palace, and it was commonly said that the Football Echo had turned white with shock.

After the first world war the Football Echo was printed on blue paper, and there were repeated requests from readers that it should return to its familiar pink. A promise was made that when Sunderland won the Cup the flush of victory would be enough to turn the editions pink. The day came in 1937, when the Roker Park club beat Preston North End at Wembley. Copies of the Football Echo were specially printed at Portsmouth as well as in Sunderland for the occasion. From Portsmouth the edition was rushed to London where 20,000 copies were sold. The "Pink 'Un" was a sign to all that Sunderland had won the Cup.

It was a great day for Sunderland—and for the Football Echo, which remained pink until April 26, 1958 when, once again it turned white with shock. When it became blue at the start of the following season we gave an undertaking that it would not resume its familiar pink colour until Sunderland returned to Division I—or won the F.A. Cup. Now that day has arrived with another "Victory Pink 'Un" to mark the club's promotion.

## Charlton's Wakeham Was The Man Of The Match

### SUNDERLAND - - - 2     CHARLTON ATHLETIC 1

SUNDERLAND received a great reception from a 50,000 crowd when they turned out for their final home game of the season against Charlton Athletic at Roker Park this afternoon. It was a welcome for the team — and a welcome back to First Division football, which was virtually assured by last week's draw with Southampton.

As there were no fitness problems, Sunderland were able to rely on an unchanged side, but Charlton changed the formation of their inside trio to bring Firmani back at centre forward.

Matthews, who has been standing in for him, switched to inside right and Peacock displaced Durandt at inside left. Conditions were ideal and there was just enough "give" in the turf to make it comfortable for the players.

Hurley lost the toss and Sunderland started the game attacking the Roker end.

**SUNDERLAND**

Montgomery

Irwin     Ashurst

Harvey    Hurley    McNab

Herd     Crossan

Usher    Sharkey    Mulhall

Ω

Glover    Firmani    Kenning

Peacock    Matthews

Edwards   Tocknell   Bailey

Kinsey     Hewie

Wakeham

**CHARLTON ATH.**

Referee: Mr W. Crossley, of Lancaster.

Sunderland won a throw on the left, and after Sharkey's centre had been cleared, Harvey broke sharply down the middle before passing out to Mulhall. The winger placed his centre well, and Usher's header from outside the far post bounced just short of the line to be hooked clear by Hewie and finally hammered oehind for a corner by Tocknell.

It was a lucky escape for Charlton, but Wakeham made no mistake when Mulhall's kick reached the middle.

### By ARGUS

#### Overhit

The first free kick came to Sunderland when Herc' was badly shaken in a tackle by Edwards. From the kick they went on to claim a corner on the right, but once again Wakeham beat everyone ir the air from Usher's kick.

Ashurst joined Mulhall in a dash down the left, but the winger
**Continued in Back Page**

## How The Teams Fared Today

### DIVISION I

| | | |
|---|---|---|
| Aston Villa 1 | Leicester C. | 3 |
| (Half-time: 1—1) | | |
| Blackburn 3 | Ipswich | 1 |
| (Half-time: 2—0) | | |
| Blackpool 2 | Sheff. Wed. | 2 |
| (Half-time: 1—1) | | |
| Chelsea 1 | Everton | 0 |
| (Half-time: 0—0) | | |
| Liverpool 5 | Arsenal | 0 |
| (Half-time: 3—0) | | |
| Notts F. 1 | Burnley | 3 |
| (Half-time: 0—2) | | |
| Sheffield U. 2 | West Brom. | 1 |
| (Half-time: 1—1) | | |
| Stoke C. 3 | Man. Utd. | 1 |
| (Half-time: 2—1) | | |
| Tottenham 1 | Bolton W. | 0 |
| (Half-time: 1—0) | | |
| Wolves 4 | Fulham | 0 |

| | P. | W. | D. | L. | F. | A. | P. |
|---|---|---|---|---|---|---|---|
| Liverpool | 39 | 26 | 4 | 9 | 92 | 37 | 56 |
| Man. Utd. | 41 | 22 | 7 | 12 | 87 | 61 | 51 |
| Everton | 41 | 20 | 10 | 11 | 83 | 64 | 50 |
| Sheffield W. | 42 | 19 | 11 | 12 | 84 | 67 | 49 |
| Chelsea | 42 | 20 | 10 | 12 | 72 | 56 | 49 |
| Tottenham | 40 | 21 | 7 | 12 | 94 | 74 | 49 |
| Blackburn | 42 | 18 | 10 | 14 | 89 | 63 | 46 |
| Arsenal | 42 | 17 | 11 | 14 | 90 | 82 | 45 |
| Sheffield Utd. | 41 | 16 | 11 | 14 | 61 | 61 | 43 |
| West Brom | 41 | 16 | 10 | 15 | 68 | 59 | 42 |
| Burnley | 41 | 16 | 10 | 15 | 64 | 62 | 42 |
| Notts For. | 41 | 16 | 9 | 16 | 63 | 68 | 41 |
| Leicester | 41 | 16 | 8 | 17 | 12 | 65 | 41 |
| West Ham U. | 41 | 14 | 12 | 15 | 68 | 72 | 40 |
| Fulham | 41 | 13 | 12 | 16 | 55 | 62 | 38 |
| Wolves | 41 | 11 | 15 | 15 | 68 | 69 | 37 |
| Blackpool | 41 | 13 | 9 | 19 | 49 | 69 | 35 |
| Stoke City | 40 | 13 | 9 | 18 | 71 | 74 | 35 |
| Aston Villa | 42 | 12 | 13 | 17 | 62 | 71 | 34 |
| Bolton W | 41 | 10 | 8 | 23 | 48 | 74 | 28 |
| Birmingham | 40 | 9 | 7 | 24 | 48 | 91 | 25 |
| Ipswich | 41 | 8 | 7 | 26 | 52 | 118 | 23 |

### DIVISION II

| | | |
|---|---|---|
| Bury | 2 | Preston NE 1 |
| (Half-time: 0—1) | | |
| Cardiff C. 2 | South'mp'n | 4 |
| (Half-time: 2—2) | | |
| Leeds U. 1 | Plymouth | 1 |
| (Half-time: 1—0) | | |
| Man. City 2 | Leyton O. | 0 |
| (Half-time: 0—0) | | |
| North'mp't 1 | Grimsby T. | 2 |
| (Half-time: 1—0) | | |
| Norwich C. 1 | Middlesbro' | 1 |
| (Half-time: 0—1) | | |
| Portsmouth 2 | Huddersf'ld | 1 |
| (Half-time: 2—1) | | |
| Rotherham 2 | Derby Co. | 0 |
| (Half-time: 1—0) | | |
| Scunthorpe 2 | Newcastle | 0 |
| (Half-time: 1—0) | | |
| Sunderland 2 | Charlton A. | 1 |
| (Half-time: 1—1) | | |
| Swindon 2 | Swansea T. | 0 |

| | P. | W. | D. | L. | F. | A. | P. |
|---|---|---|---|---|---|---|---|
| Leeds Utd. | 41 | 23 | 15 | 3 | 69 | 34 | 61 |
| Sunderland | 41 | 25 | 10 | 6 | 79 | 35 | 60 |
| Preston N.E. | 41 | 22 | 10 | 9 | 77 | 53 | 54 |
| Charlton Ath. | 41 | 18 | 16 | 12 | 76 | 68 | 48 |
| Man. City | 41 | 18 | 9 | 14 | 81 | 63 | 45 |
| Rotherham | 40 | 19 | 6 | 15 | 89 | 72 | 44 |
| Newcastle | 42 | 19 | 5 | 17 | 72 | 69 | 43 |
| Portsmouth | 40 | 16 | 10 | 14 | 77 | 66 | 42 |
| Southampton | 39 | 16 | 9 | 14 | 84 | 70 | 41 |
| Northampton | 41 | 16 | 9 | 16 | 57 | 58 | 41 |
| Middlesbreugh | 41 | 13 | 14 | 13 | 64 | 61 | 39 |
| Huddersfield | 41 | 14 | 10 | 17 | 54 | 62 | 38 |
| Swindon T. | 41 | 14 | 10 | 17 | 56 | 64 | 38 |
| Cardiff C. | 41 | 14 | 9 | 17 | 53 | 78 | 38 |
| Derby C. | 41 | 13 | 11 | 17 | 53 | 66 | 37 |
| Norwich C. | 41 | 13 | 13 | 15 | 57 | 68 | 37 |
| Leyton Or. | 41 | 13 | 9 | 19 | 53 | 71 | 35 |
| Bury | 40 | 13 | 8 | 19 | 55 | 67 | 34 |
| Swansea T. | 40 | 12 | 7 | 21 | 58 | 70 | 31 |
| Plymouth | 41 | 8 | 15 | 18 | 45 | 67 | 31 |
| Grimsby T. | 41 | 9 | 13 | 19 | 45 | 73 | 31 |
| Scunthorpe | 41 | 9 | 12 | 20 | 50 | 79 | 30 |

### DIVISION III

| | | |
|---|---|---|
| Barnsley 1 | Mansfield | 1 |
| (Half-time: 1—1) | | |
| Bournem'th 2 | Shrewsbury | 0 |
| (Half-time: 1—0) | | |
| Bristol R. 4 | Notts Co. | 0 |
| (Half-time: 2—0) | | |
| Colchester 1 | Luton T. | 1 |
| (Half-time: 1—0) | | |
| Hull C. 0 | Brentford | 0 |
| (Half-time: 0—0) | | |
| Millwall 0 | Coventry C. | 0 |
| (Half-time: 0—0) | | |
| Oldham 3 | Crewe Alex. | 2 |
| (Half-time: 1—0) | | |
| Peterboro' 1 | Crystal Pal. | 1 |
| (Half-time: 0—0) | | |
| Q.P.R. 3 | Port Vale | 0 |
| (Half-time: 1—0) | | |
| Southend 1 | Walsall | 0 |
| (Half-time: 1—0) | | |
| Watford 1 | Reading | 0 |
| (Half-time: 0—0) | | |
| Wrexham 1 | Bristol C. | 1 |

| | P. | W. | D. | L. | F. | A. | P. |
|---|---|---|---|---|---|---|---|
| Crystal Palace | 44 | 23 | 13 | 8 | 70 | 46 | 59 |
| Coventry C. | 44 | 21 | 16 | 7 | 97 | 59 | 58 |
| Watford | 44 | 23 | 11 | 10 | 76 | 55 | 57 |
| Bournemouth | 44 | 23 | 8 | 13 | 75 | 55 | 54 |
| Bristol C. | 44 | 18 | 15 | 11 | 80 | 63 | 51 |
| Mansfield T. | 43 | 19 | 11 | 14 | 71 | 59 | 49 |
| Reading | 44 | 19 | 10 | 15 | 70 | 58 | 48 |
| Oldham A. | 44 | 18 | 9 | 17 | 70 | 68 | 46 |
| Bristol R. | 44 | 19 | 8 | 17 | 88 | 70 | 46 |
| Shrewsbury | 44 | 17 | 11 | 16 | 68 | 78 | 45 |
| Hull C. | 44 | 17 | 12 | 15 | 61 | 41 | 46 |
| Peterborough | 44 | 17 | 11 | 16 | 72 | 68 | 45 |
| Southend | 44 | 14 | 15 | 15 | 73 | 73 | 43 |
| Port Vale | 44 | 14 | 13 | 16 | 48 | 49 | 43 |
| Brentford | 43 | 15 | 12 | 16 | 83 | 62 | 42 |
| Colchester | 44 | 11 | 19 | 14 | 69 | 67 | 41 |
| Q.P.R. | 42 | 17 | 6 | 19 | 68 | 73 | 40 |
| Millwall | 44 | 14 | 12 | 18 | 51 | 53 | 40 |
| Walsall | 44 | 12 | 14 | 18 | 57 | 73 | 38 |
| Luton Town | 43 | 14 | 9 | 20 | 60 | 78 | 37 |
| Barnsley | 43 | 12 | 12 | 19 | 65 | 91 | 36 |
| Crewe Alex. | 44 | 10 | 12 | 22 | 46 | 73 | 32 |
| Wrexham | 44 | 13 | 5 | 26 | 73 | 100 | 31 |
| Notts Co. | 44 | 9 | 8 | 27 | 42 | 86 | 26 |

### North Reg. League

| | | |
|---|---|---|
| Grimsby T. 1 | Hull C. | 0 |
| Doncaster R 2 | Darlington | 4 |
| Middlesbro' 4 | Gateshead | 1 |
| Stockport 0 | Scunthorpe | 0 |
| Workington 1 | Lincoln C. | 0 |

### F.A. Amateur Cup Final

| | | |
|---|---|---|
| Crook T. 2 | Enfield | 1 |

### Scottish League: Div. 1

| | | |
|---|---|---|
| Aberdeen 0 | Dundee U. | 0 |
| (Half-time: 0—0) | | |
| Airdrie 2 | St Mirren | 4 |
| (Half-time: 1—2) | | |
| Celtic 1 | Hearts | 1 |
| (Half-time: 1—1) | | |
| Dundee 5 | Partick Th. | 2 |
| (Half-time: 3—0) | | |
| Falkirk 3 | Queen of S. | 2 |
| (Half-time: 2—0) | | |
| Hibernian 5 | E. Stirling | 2 |
| (Half-time: 2—2) | | |
| Kilmarnock 4 | St Johnst'ne | 1 |
| (Half-time: 2—1) | | |
| Rangers 5 | Motherwell | 1 |
| (Half-time: 0—1) | | |
| Th. Lanark 0 | Dunfermline | 1 |

### Scottish League: Div. 2

| | | |
|---|---|---|
| Alloa 2 | Dumbarton | 1 |
| (Half-time: 1—1) | | |
| Arbroath 2 | East Fife | 3 |
| (Half-time: 1—1) | | |
| Berwick R. 4 | Queen's Pk | 2 |
| (Half-time: 1—1) | | |
| Cowdenb'th 1 | Morton | 5 |
| (Half-time: 1—3) | | |
| Hamilton 3 | Brechin | 3 |
| (Half-time: 2—2) | | |
| Montrose 3 | Albion R. | 4 |
| (Half-time: 2—2) | | |
| Raith R. 1 | Forfar Ath. | 4 |
| (Half-time: 1—2) | | |
| Stirling Alb. 0 | Stenh'sem'r | 2 |
| (Half-time: 0—1) | | |
| Stranraer 3 | Clyde | 1 |
| (Half-time: 3—1) | | |

*Sunderland narrowly missed out on promotion to the First Division in 1962 and 1963 but they finally returned to the big time in 1964.*

Average home attendance: 42,874

*Following Sunderland's return to top flight football, Argus' Roker Reflections column in the Sunderland Football Echo rounded off the season in optimistic note. "Six years after they bowed out of the First Division for the first time in the club's history, Sunderland are going back to prove all over again their entitlement to a place in the top sphere of British soccer. Second Division clubs, quick with their congratulations are sorry to see them go; First Division clubs welcome them back warmly. For their part, Sunderland are relieved that it is all over and, behind the spirit of celebrations sparked off by last week's triumph over Charlton Athletic, there is firstly the realisation that it will be an exacting business keeping the boom going next season and secondly no lack of confidence that it can be done. Every player on Sunderland's books is now rated a man with a future and additions to that group must be of top material."*

### F.A. Cup (Sixth Round Replay) 1963-1964

## SUNDERLAND 2 MANCHESTER UNITED 2 (after extra time)

Over the two hours, Sunderland carved out the better chances and it was disappointing that they could only accept two of them. Manchester United crammed their best efforts into brief spasms which often called for desperate rearguard action by Hurley and his defence. Sunderland's best chance in the first half came after Mulhall's header from a long ball by Hurley had been headed out of the middle. It was returned to Sharkey whose scissor kick from the edge of the penalty area flashed out of Gaskell's reach and just inside the far post to put Sunderland one goal up at the interval.

Sunderland should have increased their lead early in the second half when Crossan intercepted a back pass from Charlton. With only the goalkeeper to beat, he side-stepped Gaskell but slipped in the process giving the keeper the chance to recover. Shortly afterwards, Manchester United were gifted an equaliser when Montgomery mis-hit his goal kick and when the ball travelled straight to Law on the edge of the penalty area, he made no mistake. Shortly afterwards, Manchester United could have taken the lead when a Best centre just scraped clear of Law and Charlton who were both menacingly placed in front of goal. That was to be the last real chance of the half and the game proceeded into extra-time.

Within seconds of the re-start, Sunderland were ahead. When Harvey hit a low pass to Sharkey, the youngster first-timed it into the middle for George Herd but Setters got their first only to slide the ball past his own goalkeeper. The game maintained an incredible pace throughout extra-time with Sunderland enjoying the best of the play although they were lucky not to concede a goal when a fierce shot from Law beat Montgomery and came back from the underside of the bar. It appeared that Sunderland were heading for a famous victory when David Herd gained possession on the right and centred for Charlton to score a great equaliser.

**Sunderland:** Montgomery, Irwin, Ashurst, Harvey, Hurley, Elliott, Usher, Herd, Sharkey, Crossan, Mulhall.

**Manchester United:** Gaskell, Brennan, Dunne, Crerand, Foulkes, Setters, Herd, Chisnall, Charlton, Law, Best.

# 1964-1965

Sunderland's preparation for their return to top flight football could hardly have been worse. Alan Brown's surprising decision to resign as manager rocked the club during the close season. Having spent seven seasons sorting out the club's problems at all levels, his decision to walk away from the club at the very moment promotion was secured remains one of soccer's greatest mysteries. Whatever Mr Brown's reasons were, the stark reality of the situation was that Sunderland re-entered the First Division arena without a manager.

To add to Sunderland's tale of woe, goalkeeper Jimmy Montgomery, who had been a tower of strength during the promotion season, injured a hand during pre season training and missed the first thirteen games of the season. His deputy for the opening game of the season against Leicester City was Derek Forster who at 15 years and 185 days old became the youngest goalkeeper to play in the Football League and the second youngest player to play anywhere in the First Division.

In contrast to their tremendous away record during the promotion season, Sunderland lost their first eleven away games and won just one of their first fifteen games.

It was not until 14th November 1964 that a successor to Alan Brown was appointed and this was George Hardwick. On the day of his appointment, Sunderland won their second game of the season; a 3-2 home victory against Burnley. They also won their next two games at Roker Park against Everton (4 0) and Chelsea (3-0). They even managed to sneak a 1-0 away win at Leicester City before the end of the year but their away form generally remained poor.

Sunderland's home form under George Hardwick was most encouraging; eleven victories from fourteen games and it was from their efforts at Roker Park that a position of mid table respectability was achieved at the season's end.

In the F.A. Cup, Sunderland survived an away tie at Luton Town but fell at the next hurdle, a home game against one of the First Division's leading lights — Nottingham Forest. In the League Cup there were emphatic 4-1 home wins against both West Ham United and Blackpool but Sunderland's interest in the competition was terminated for another season with a 4-2 defeat at Coventry City.

Amazingly, after he had guided Sunderland to First Division safety long before the end of the season and from a most precarious position in November, George Hardwick was sacked as manager. Sunderland were all set to enter one of the most depressing periods in their illustrious history.

**Incoming players included:**
Alan Black, Billy Campbell, Derek Forster, Alan Gauden, Mike Hellawell, Harry Hood, Sandy McLaughlan, John O'Hare, John Parke

**Outgoing players included:**
Brian Clough, Johnny Crossan, Colin Nelson.

**Sunderland's league record read:**

| P | W | D | L | F | A | Pts | Position |
|---|---|---|---|---|---|-----|----------|
| 42 | 14 | 9 | 19 | 64 | 74 | 37 | 15th |

League appearances (with F.A. Cup and League Cup appearances in brackets): Ashurst 39 (5), Black 2, Campbell 3, Clough 3, Crossan 16 (2), Elliott 5 (1), Foster 3, Harvey 38 (4), Hellawell 14, Herd 39 (5), Hood 24 (1), Hurley 27 (2), Irwin 19 (2), McLaughlan 30 (3), McNab 37 (4), Mitchinson 10 (4), Montgomery 9 (2), Moore 2, Mulhall 41 (5), Nelson 1 (1), O'Hare 5 (2), Parke 24 (2), Rooks 16 (4), Sharkey 32 (3), Slack 2, Usher 20 (3).

Average home attendance: 39,140.

*George Herd had been a Sunderland target for some time when Alan Brown finally secured his transfer on 27th April 1961.*

*Argus' first summary of a First Division Football season for six years sounded a note of caution when he wrote in the Sunderland Football Echo, "The season now ending has brought both a reprieve and a warning for Sunderland. I do not think it is any exaggeration to say that the club's standing for years ahead may well be shaped by the decisions which will have to be taken in the course of the next few months. The reprieve was the reward for a desperately hard effort by the team at the crucial stage of the season. It was a fighting effort and the greatest credit is due to the players who pulled out the extra to make it possible. But they then slipped back into the disordered groove in which they slumped towards trouble in the early months of the season. We are left with the thought that the team played above itself to meet a crisis and, the crisis over, immediately reverted to average. If this is indeed the average then the team is not good enough by a long way. Survival in the First Division is not enough. The club and its supporters walked the tightrope at the bottom of the First Division for most of the seasons after the war and by the time they were overtaken by the inevitable, they were an impoverished club both financially and in terms of playing strength. The same uninspiring outlook which made safety a bigger prize than success must not be allowed to command the scene again."*

# 1965-1966

Ian McColl arrived as manager and in his first season in control took Sunderland to the brink of relegation and reduced the average home attendance by almost 6,000 in the process.

Sunderland could manage only one away victory all season and were knocked out of the F.A. Cup in the third round by Everton who won convincingly 3-0. A 2-1 triumph against Sheffield United in the first round of the League Cup was followed by a 2-1 defeat against Aston Villa at Roker Park.

Major signings included Jim Baxter from Rangers and Neil Martin from Hibernian as Mr McColl attempted to re-shape the Sunderland team.

**Incoming players included:**
Jim Baxter, Billy Hughes, Bobby Kerr, Neil Martin, Malcolm Moore, Colin Todd.

**Outgoing players included:**
Norman Clarke, Willie McPheat, Tommy Mitchinson, Dickie Rooks, Mel Slack, Brian Usher.

**Sunderland's league record read:**

| P | W | D | L | F | A | Pts | Position |
|---|---|---|---|---|---|-----|----------|
| 42 | 14 | 8 | 20 | 51 | 72 | 36 | 19th |

League appearances (with F.A. Cup and League Cup appearances in brackets): Ashurst 37 (3), Baxter 35 (3), Black 2, Campbell 2, Elliott 12 (1), Gauden 14 (1), Harvey 39 (3), Hellawell 28 (2), Herd 37 (3), Hurley 24 (1), Irwin 29 (1), Martin 24 (1), McLaughlan 13, McNab 28 (3), Mitchinson 3, Montgomery 29 (3), Moore 8 (1), Mulhall 35 (2), O'Hare 17, Parke 31 (3), Sharkey 15 (2).

Average home attendance: 33,159

*Scottish international George Mulhall who was signed by Alan Brown from Aberdeen for a fee of £25,000 in 1962.*

*"Sunderland's return to the First Division, acclaimed so warmly two years ago, has fallen well below the promise which it held out to success starved supporters," commented Argus in his end of season summing up in the Sunderland Football Echo. Argus continued, "Instead of the continued surge towards right of entry into European competition, we have had two seasons of struggle to retain First Division status. The invitation to look ahead confidently has been weakening all the time. Indeed, the end of the season at Roker Park this afternoon would come as something of a relief to supporters who have seen so much in-and-out form since last August that their sense of loyalty has been severley shaken"*

## 1966-1967

Once again, Sunderland finished the season with thirty six points but this time two places higher in the league table at seventeenth. Unlike the previous season, any fears of relegation were dispelled well before the end of the season but that did not disguise the fact that results were far from satisfactory. Although Sunderland's form at home was reasonable at times, away results were nothing short of appalling with only two victories all season and a string of worrying defeats including 5-0 at both Manchester United and Sheffield Wednesday.

There were some encouraging performances in the F.A. Cup with emphatic victories against Brentford (5-2) and Peterborough United (7-1) before the reward of a home tie with Leeds United. A crowd of 55,763 attended Roker Park to see Neil Martin put Sunderland ahead although the game ended in a 1-1 draw to set up a replay at Elland Road. Once again the game produced a 1-1 draw with John O'Hare scoring Sunderland's goal. The second replay saw Sunderland lose 2-1 in highly controversial circumstances. After Alan Gauden scored for Sunderland, the game was heading into extra time when Cecil Irwin was judged to have tripped Greenhoff in the penalty box. Leeds United scored from the resulting penalty through Giles with George Herd and George Mulhall being dismissed by the referee for leading the protests. Most observers felt that Greenhoff had dived and that the alleged foul had taken place outside the penalty area.

In the League Cup, Sunderland's involvement was short lived, losing to Sheffield United in a second round replay.

**Incoming players included:**
George Kinnell, Colin Suggett.

**Outgoing players included:**
Alan Black, Harry Campbell, Dave Elliott, Mike Hellawell, Harry Hood, Jimmy McNab, Gary Moore, Dominick Sharkey.

**Sunderland's league record read:**

| P | W | D | L | F | A | Pts | Position |
|---|---|---|---|---|---|-----|----------|
| 42 | 14 | 8 | 20 | 58 | 72 | 36 | 17th |

League appearances (with F.A. Cup and League Cup appearances in brackets)
Ashurst 28 (2), Baxter 36 (6), Elliott 8, Gauden 24 (4), Harvey 28 (7), Hellawell 1, Herd 35 (7), Hurley 11, Hood 7 (1), Hughes 6, Irwin 41 (7), Kerr 8 (3), Kinnell 29 (5), Martin 41 (7), McNab 14 (2) Montgomery 42, Moore 3, Mulhall 33 (7), O'Hare 29 (6), Parke 7, Sharkey 2, Shoulder 3, Suggett 5, Todd 21 (6)

Average home attendance: 32,631

*George Kinnell leads the team out at Roker Park during 1966-1967 season. He was signed from Oldham Athletic for £20,000 by manager Ian McColl in October 1966.*

*In his end of season summary of events on the pitch, Argus wrote in the Sunderland Football Echo, "Success is the only yardstick which counts with the majority of supporters and they are entitled to look back on the failures of this season now ending and feel that the fare to which they are entitled is still passing them by. Instead of the promised excitement, returning to the First Division has, in many respects, meant little more than a return to the pre-relegation era, with all its anxieties. The clear road ahead which emerged at the end of six years' servitude in the Second Division has, for the moment, petered out and its replacement has not even begun to take shape. Yet the discerning ones will agree that the team which finished this season has a higher potential than those which played out time in the two previous seasons. To that extent at least, progress has been made. If the obvious gaps can be filled by the current drive for players, then things could begin to take a turn for the better."*

The F.A. Cup fifth round, second replay against Leeds United ended in highly controversial circumstances. The game, which is reported on the next page, brought the following after match quotes:-

Don Revie (Leeds United Manager): "It was unfortunate that the game had to end with such incidents. I thought, though, that we played better than in the first replay last Wednesday."

Lord Harwood (Leeds United President): "I thought we were lucky to win. Yes, you can say we were lucky."

Ian McColl (Sunderland Manager): "We are considering making a protest about the penalty. It was rubbish. Greenhoff was a mile offside and even then it was very doubtful whether Irwin fouled him."

Joe Sime (flat race jockey): "It was just like being beaten by a short head."

Boothferry Park, Hull was the venue for a game which Sunderland lost as a result of some disgraceful refereeing decisions made by World Cup referee Ken Stokes.

Leeds United could have been ahead in the first minute when Giles charged down a Todd clearance but as he moved through the middle, Harvey intercepted. However, Sunderland did go behind ten minutes later when Giles hit a free kick into the penalty area and with two Leeds players charging into the area, Montgomery could only push the ball out and when it came to Lorimer his hard drive rebounded from the post to Belfitt to score an easy goal. The remainder of the half was played hard and fast but without either side being able to gain advantage in front of goal.

The second half showed Leeds United as the cynical, provocative side with all the Revie hallmarks and it was amazing that several of their tackles should go unpunished, only for Irwin to be booked in the 76th minute for an alleged foul on Cooper. Two minutes later Sunderland were level when Gauden hammered the ball through a bunch of players on the edge of the penalty area and into the net. The next twelve minutes saw an onslaught on the Leeds goal as Mulhall O'Hare, Martin and Gauden all pulverised the Leeds' defence. With extra-time looking likely, a fierce tackle by Charlton on O'Hare was astonishingly ignored by the referee and the ball was played to Greenhoff who was well offside. Playing to the whistle, Irwin made a clean tackle on Greenhoff when the referee made a mockery of his World Cup ranking by awarding a penalty. Giles took the kick and with Mongomery diving the wrong way Leeds were back in front. When George Herd and George Mulhall headed the Sunderland protests, referee Stokes sent them off. Sunderland did go through the motions of protesting but the 2-1 scoreline remained.

**Sunderland:** Montgomery, Irwin, Harvey, Todd, Kinnell, Baxter, Gauden, O'Hare, Martin, Herd, Mulhall.

**Leeds United:** Sprake, Reaney, Bell, Bremner, Charlton, Hunter, Lorimer, Belfitt, Greenhoff, Giles, Cooper.

# 1967-1968

The bright spots of the season included the emergence of Colin Todd and Colin Suggett as regular first team players with tremendous potential. However, results did not improve and a sequence of ten games without a win stretching from mid November to the end of January set the alarm bells ringing around Roker Park. Although Sunderland's away record improved to the extent of five victories, their home form worsened.

In the League Cup, victories against Halifax Town and Everton were followed by a home defeat by Leeds United while the F.A. Cup exit at home to Second Division Norwich City was followed by the departure of manager Ian McColl and the subsequent return of Alan Brown.

Ironically, Mr Brown's first game in charge since re-joining the club took him back to Hillsborough where a Ralph Brand goal secured both points for Sunderland. However, the next four games were all lost before Sunderland saw an upturn in form which included three away wins and an end of season position of fifteenth.

**Incoming players included:**
Ralph Brand, Geoff Butler, Brian Chambers, Gordon Harris, Brian Heslop, Richard Huntley, Paddy Lowery, Calvin Palmer, Ian Porterfield, Bruce Stuckey, Dennis Tueart.

**Outgoing players included:**
Jim Baxter, Neil Martin, Sandy McLaughlan, John O'Hare.

**Sunderland's league record read:**

| P | W | D | L | F | A | Pts | Position |
|---|---|---|---|---|---|-----|----------|
| 42 | 13 | 11 | 18 | 51 | 61 | 37 | 15th |

League appearances (with F.A. Cup and League Cup appearances in brackets) Ashurst 22 (1), Baxter 16 (2), Brand 28 (1), Butler 1 (2), Forster 3, Gauden 2, Harris 14, Harvey 23 (2), Herd 28 (3), Heslop 15 (3), Hughes 5 (2), Hurley 20 (3), Irwin 27, Kinnell 35 (5), Martin 21 (5), Montgomery 39 (5), Moore 2, Mulhall 33 (4), Palmer 7, Parke 21 (3), Porterfield 8 (2), Stuckey 8 (1), Suggett 42 (5), Todd 42 (4).

Average home attendance: 30,181

*Colin Suggett was one of the outstanding successes of Alan Brown's youth policy. He made his first team debut under manager Ian McColl in 1966-1967 season.*

*Despite sitting through a season of turmoil and failure, Argus could find justification for some close season optimism when he wrote in the Sunderland Football Echo, "Because of the strange pattern of events which has surrounded the club since the war, Sunderland supporters have become much more inclined to look ahead... and they have usually had little joy in doing so. Now that another season has run its full course, the events of the 1967-1968 season will come under review and one wonders whether they will find enough encouragement in the trends which it reveals to break with practice and begin to look ahead hopefully. The invitation to do so is there and though it is anybody's guess whether the climb back towards the top will be a long slow haul or a comparatively sharp surge, the certainty is that at long last the right atmosphere for progress has been achieved and there are early signs of development on a broad front. Events themselves pay the greatest possible tribute to the part which manager Alan Brown has played in shaping a new outlook throughout the club. It may be argued that the trend towards better times started a little earlier from the decision to give up the idea of trying to build a team around Jim Baxter and accepting the £100,000 fee which Nottingham Forest were so anxious to pay. After thirty months of failure the time for fresh thinking had certainly arrived. Since Mr Brown arrived at the club for a second term of office, there have been few outward signs of change but the quiet revolution within the club, based on a new set of values, gave the team back its fighting heart and dovetailed known strengths into a team pattern which deserved to succeed. There is still a lot of hard work to be done but Mr Brown has pulled his staff together into a team ready to accept responsibility and eager for the rewards which success can bring."*

# 1968-1969

Once again, Sunderland spent the entire season at the wrong end of the table. One away win all season equalled an all-time-worst record while a total of ten wins at home was barely acceptable. Long suffering travelling supporters were made to suffer a trio of dismal performances in the capital with away defeats at West Ham (8-0), Chelsea (5-1) and Tottenham Hotspur (5-1).

The London jinx also struck in both cup competitions with Sunderland suffering immediate exits in the F.A. Cup and League Cup after meeting Fulham (4-1 home defeat) and Arsenal (1-0 away defeat) respectively.

Sunderland finished the season just four points clear of a relegation position and with an alarming slump in attendances at Roker Park.

The Sports Final edition of the Sunderland Echo on 17th May 1969 broke the news that the club was severing long term links with several players in order to pave the way for a new framework at all levels for the 1969-1970 season. The most significant moves involved the granting of free transfers to Charlie Hurley and George Mulhall.

**Incoming players included:**
Keith Coleman, John Lathan, Mick McGiven, Fred McIver, Bobby Park, Ritchie Pitt, John Tones.

**Outgoing players included:**
Geoff Butler, Alan Gauden, George Kinnell, John Parke.

**Sunderland's league record read:**

| P | W | D | L | F | A | Pts | Position |
|---|---|---|---|---|---|-----|----------|
| 42 | 11 | 12 | 19 | 43 | 67 | 34 | 17th |

League appearances (with F.A. Cup and League Cup appearances in brackets): Ashurst 17, Brand 3, Harris 39 (2), Harvey 37 (2), Herd 24 (1), Heslop 13, Hughes 24 (2), Huntley 1, Hurley 33 (2), Irwin 25 (1), Kerr 15 (1), Kinnell 3, Lowrey 3, Montgomery 42 (2), Moore 8, Mulhall 30, Porterfield 22 (2), Palmer 23, Pitt 7, Stuckey 6 (1), Suggett 36 (2), Todd 41 (2), Tueart 10 (1).

*Dennis Tueart and Calvin Palmer in 1969.*

Average home attendance: 25,514

*Argus summed up the 1968-1969 season in realistic fashion when he wrote, "The 1968-1969 season will be remembered as a period in which supporters, as well as results, had Sunderland Football Club facing up to unpleasant and unpalatable facts. The downward swing which started shortly after promotion has continued and it has still to be proved whether the decline has been arrested. Better use of the tremendous financial resources which flowed into the club during the first four years of that period could have produced a brighter picture of the post promotion era. By the time the brakes went on, the task of checking the slide has had to be tackled without the luxury of going into the transfer market as buyers. The last time Sunderland went a full season without buying was in 1963-1964 when they won promotion but the chance of them making comparable impact from existing staff this time was never on. The average home attendance is the second lowest for the post war period. This is the verdict of the paying customers who have exercised their right to register their protest in the manner which is felt most keenly."*

# 1969-1970

In short, this was Sunderland's worst season in their eighty year history. Results were nothing short of disgraceful and with just six victories all season, relegation was inevitable. Ever since promotion six years earlier, Sunderland's life in the First Division had been one long struggle and failure to wisely invest the significant revenue from the turnstiles in team building meant that Sunderland were destined for another spell in the Second Division wilderness.

Sunderland took a mere three points from their first ten games and their goal scoring achievements of just seventeen goals at home all season set an unenviable record. The previous season's leading goal scorer Colin Suggett (with nine goals!) had been sold to West Bromwich Albion for £100,000 during the close season and he had been replaced at the top of the goal scoring charts by Gordon Harris with seven goals (including three penalties!).

With such an appalling league record it came as no surprise, when the team suffered immediate exits from both domestic cup competitions. Third Division Bradford City ended Sunderland's interest in the League Cup for another season with a 2-1 win at Roker Park while Sunderland saw their F.A. Cup hopes evaporate at Filbert Street when Leicester City from the Second Division ran out 1-0 victors.

**Incoming players included:**
Joe Baker, Mick Horswill, Colin Symm.

**Outgoing players included:**
Ralph Brand, George Herd, Richard Huntley, Charlie Hurley, George Mulhall, Jimmy Shoulder, Colin Suggett.

**Sunderland's league record read:**

| P | W | D | L | F | A | Pts | Position |
|---|---|---|---|---|---|-----|----------|
| 42 | 6 | 14 | 22 | 30 | 68 | 26 | 21st |

League appearances (with F.A. Cup and League Cup appearances in brackets): Ashurst 31 (2), Baker 24 (2), Harris 39 (2), Harvey 19 (2), Heslop 28 (2), Hughes 33 (1), Irwin 32 (1), Kerr 21, Lathan 5, Lowrey 1, McGiven 42 (1), Montgomery 41 (2), Palmer 5 (1), Park 26 (1), Pitt 17 (1), Stuckey 10 (1), Symm 7, Todd 40 (1), Tueart 38 (2).

Average home attendance: 21,295

*Joe Baker cost Sunderland a modest £30,000 when he was signed from Nottingham Forest in June 1969.*

*Argus summed up a sad season for everyone connected with Sunderland Football club when he wrote in the final Sunderland Football Echo of the season, "Today's position is the full penalty for failure to give the constant need for team improvements absolute priority. The change to a more realistic course of action cannot come quickly enough, though it could take several years to repair the damage which has been done. It is a fact that at one time, twenty five per cent of the money paid at the gate was ploughed back into the team but this has now slumped to five per cent. And it is five per cent of a rapidly decreasing sum. The prosperity of a club is both governed and indicated by the number of spectators which it can attract to watch the team in action. The long road which Sunderland have travelled since 1950 is shown by the fact that support has dwindled from over a million in the 1949-1950 season for the first and only time in the club's history to an all-time low of 457,000 in the current campaign."*

## Division 1 1969-1970 — SUNDERLAND 1   NEWCASTLE UNITED 1

Sunderland were grateful for the point salvaged against an impressive Newcastle United. The Roker side were thankful for the brilliance of Montgomery in goal and relied upon a lot of hard running to contain Newcastle in the first half which the visitors largely dominated. For United, Robson and Dyson threatened to score an avalanche of goals and at times the Sunderland defence were at full stretch to keep them out.

Despite taking the lead through Smith in the 51st minute, Newcastle's command on the game weakened in the second half. The visitors goal resulted from a break by Burton upfield from which his centre was eventually met by Dyson. There were no takers in the middle and when the ball broke to the far angle of the penalty area, Smith cracked a right foot shot towards goal to give Montgomery no chance. In the 75th minute, Sunderland's committment to attack finally paid dividends. Tueart set up Park in front of goal and when his shot came back from the bar Tueart dived in bravely to put the ball into the net out of the reach of McFaul. Both sides had opportunities to win the game but in the end a draw was probably a fair result.

**Sunderland:** Montgomery, Irwin, Harvey, Todd, Heslop, McGiven, Park, Kerr, Hughes, Harris and Tueart.

**Newcastle United:** McFaul, Craig, Guthrie, Gibb, Burton, Moncur, Robson, Dyson, Davies, Smith and Foggon.

# 1970-1971

This was one of the most depressing seasons in the history of Sunderland A.F.C. The abysmal performances of the team were reflected in the Roker Park attendances which plummeted to an average of 15,869 — the lowest recorded in post-war years. By the end of the season, of the forty four contracted players, only four had cost the club a transfer fee. The four players concerned were Gordon Harris, Dick Malone, Ian Porterfield and Dave Watson.

At no stage during the season did Sunderland put together a good run of results to suggest the remotest possibility of promotion. Indeed, a depressing run during the second half of the season in which Sunderland failed to register a single victory in eight games and score just one goal, set alarm bells ringing at the other end of the table.

The club eventually finished in the lower half of the table in thirteenth position during a season which saw their instant dismissal from both the League Cup (to Lincoln City who finished the season applying for re-election to the Fourth Division) and the F.A. Cup (in a game which they lost 3-0 at home to Orient).

**Incoming players included:**
Jackie Ashurst, Maurice Hepworth, Dick Malone, Trevor Swinburne, Dave Watson.

**Outgoing players included:**
Len Ashurst, Joe Baker, Brian Heslop, Malcolm Moore, Calvin Palmer, Bruce Stuckey, Colin Todd.

**Sunderland's league record read:**

| P | W | D | L | F | A | Pts | Position |
|---|---|---|---|---|---|-----|----------|
| 42 | 15 | 12 | 15 | 52 | 54 | 42 | 13th |

League appearances (with F.A. Cup and League Cup appearances in brackets): Baker 15 (2), Chambers 17 (1), Harris 30 (2), Harvey 40 (2), Hepworth 2, Heslop 1, Hughes 39 (2), Irwin 36 (2), Kerr 38 (2), Lathan 1, Lowrey 7, Malone 21, McGiven 15 (1), Montgomery 42 (2), Park 23 (2), Pitt 36 (1), Porterfield 37 (2), Tueart 19, Todd 26 (1), Watson 17.

Average home attendance: 15,869

*Colin Todd was one of Sunderland's finest defenders. He played 170 games for Sunderland before being transferred to Derby County for £175,000 in 1971.*

*Argus' end of season analysis in the Sunderland Football Echo was optimistic in the extreme and was certainly at odds with the opinions of the majority of supporters when he wrote, "Though there must be a sense of disappointment over the fact that their one-time supporters decided, or were pursuaded, to desert them in increasing numbers, Sunderland can still look back on the 1970 1971 seasons as a fruitful period in which they made progress against the odds. It was always realised that it would be a difficult first season down in the Second Division and the task was to consolidate as quickly as possible and then prepare the way for a push towards the top. A comfortable mid table position indicates that Sunderland have been no better than an average Second Division side. I still believe that this one season — at least — in the Second Division will prove to be of the greatest value in the development of the team up to the level where supporters will come flooding back to launch Sunderland into another era of success."*

# 1971-1972

There were less than ten thousand people inside Roker Park for the opening game of the season against Birmingham City. With the previous season being one of the worst in the club's history and no money being made available to manager Alan Brown for close season team strengthening, it was no surprise when supporters decided to vote with their feet.

The second version of Alan Brown's youth policy was starting to take shape with Bobby Park, Ritchie Pitt, Mick McGiven, Billy Hughes, Dennis Tueart, John Lathan, Paddy Lowery, Jimmy Hamilton, Brian Chambers, Keith Coleman and Fred McIver all graduating to the first team during the opening weeks of the season.

Jimmy Hamilton's debut for Sunderland in the 4-1 home victory against Middlesbrough gave him the distinction of becoming Sunderland's youngest first team player at 16 years and 103 days.

With Alan Brown's second youth policy well under way, results in the minor leagues were most encouraging. Sunderland's reserve team topped the North Midlands League at the end of the season with 43 points from 28 games thanks to some outstanding performances by the likes of Colin Beesley, Maurice Hepworth, Mick Horswill, Paddy Lowrey, Fred McIver, Colin Symm and John Tones.

The youth team also finished the season in pole position in the Northern Intermediate league. The team won 25 of their 30 games, accumulated 52 points and finished the season with a staggering 75 goals scored and just 29 conceded.

When Sunderland won four out of five games between mid September and early October, promotion hopes were again fuelled. However, a subsequent run of just one victory in the next ten games put paid to any mid season celebrations, although a late season run of seven games without defeat contributed to a final league position of fifth.

In the League Cup, Sunderland played just one game, losing to Bristol Rovers at Eastville. The F.A. Cup brought a convincing 3-0 win against Sheffield Wednesday and a three game epic against Cardiff City which the Welshman eventually won in a second replay at Maine Road.

**Incoming players included:**
Joe Bolton, Jimmy Hamilton

**There were no senior outgoing players.**

**Sunderland's league record read:**

| P | W | D | L | F | A | Pts | Position |
|---|---|---|---|---|---|-----|----------|
| 42 | 17 | 16 | 9 | 67 | 57 | 50 | 5th |

League appearances (with F.A. Cup and League Cup appearances in brackets): Bolton 4, Chambers 25 (3), Coleman 32 (4), Forster 11 (1), Hamilton 4, Harris 2, Harvey 31 (5), Horswill 7, Hughes 21 (5), Irwin 4 (1), Kerr 39 (5), Lathan 12, Lowery 2, Malone 41 (5), McGiven 32 (1), McIver 1, Montgomery 31 (4), Park 1, Pitt 41 (5), Porterfield 36 (5), Symm 2 (1), Tueart 40 (5), Watson 42 (5)

*Dick Malone who was signed from Ayr United in 1970 and took over from Cecil Irwin at right back.*

Average home attendance: 17,282

*"Exciting Progress On Broadest Of Fronts" was the bold statement made by Argus in the Sunderland Football Echo upon the conclusion of the 1971-1972 season. Little did anyone know then that Argus' words of optimism for the future would, in the F.A. Cup at least, be spot on. Argus continued, "The 16,000 regular supporters who have followed the Sunderland team this season will have no doubt that this has been a season of significant progress which points the way ahead and promises a swift return to an overdue era of success. When Mr. Alan Brown predicted that Sunderland would have as good a chance as anyone of winning the Second Division championship, it seemed a bold forecast but it was in many respects an understatement, for with nine games to play they had a better chance than all except Norwich City of lifting the big prize. However, the squandering of home points in three successive games knocked them right out of the running. There is a difference of opinion on whether it would have been a good thing to claim promotion this season in view of the lack of maturity of several of the players who have played important roles. Young players have taken over key positions and distinguished themselves; the supply lines between youth, reserve and senior teams having been shortened dramatically. It is an exciting prospect that these players will be far better equipped next season to launch a promotion challenge and to prepare for the bigger tasks which lie ahead if they manage to command success in their drive."*

# 1972-1973

Sunderland started well with twelve points from the season's first six away games and four home games. A decline followed, beginning with a 5-1 defeat at Oxford followed by further defeats at home to Luton and away to Q.P.R.

Following a lethargic goalless draw at home to Fulham before a paltry crowd of 11,618, Alan Brown left the club on 1st November 1972 and was replaced four weeks later by Bob Stokoe. In the interim period, Billy Elliott had acted as caretaker manager and although the team only managed to win two and lose two games under his guidance, one tactical move of Elliott's was to be instrumental in Sunderland's subsequent improvement in form. Alan Brown had signed Dave Watson from Rotherham United in December 1970 as a centre forward to replace Joe Baker. Watson played eighty one games in Sunderland's number nine shirt, scoring nineteen goals. He failed to score in any of his thirteen games in the 1972-1973 season up to the time of Alan Brown's departure. In a tactical switch, Elliott moved Watson to centre half and such was the success of the move that he remained there for the rest of his distinguished career.

Bob Stokoe's first game in charge brought a 1-0 home defeat by Burnley on 2nd December but the club lost only a further five league games all season during which time they soared from a relegation position to sixth in the table. Stokoe achieved this astonishing turnabout with a minumum outlay in the transfer market. Only Ron Guthrie and Vic Halom of the short-term signings had contributed to the transformation.

Although the club's interest in the League Cup under Alan Brown had been short lived thanks to a 3-0 defeat by Stoke City at the first hurdle, performance in the F.A. Cup under Bob Stokoe more than made up for the disappointment!

Sunderland's F.A. Cup adventure under Bob Stokoe started at Meadow Lane where the team forced a 1-1 draw thanks to a goal from striker turned defender Dave Watson. A further goal from Watson together with one from Dennis Tueart disposed of Notts County in the replay at Roker Park to set up a fourth round tie with Reading. Disappointingly, Sunderland were held to a 1-1 draw at Roker Park with Dennis Tueart scoring once again. The replay at Elm Park was won in convincing style 3-1 with goals from Kerr, Watson and Tueart. The fifth round presented Sunderland with a much more formidable task; an away tie at First Division Manchester City. Already, many Sunderland fans had the famous twin towers of Wembley firmly in their sights and there was actually a feeling of anti-climax when the game ended in a draw – a fantastic result in retrospect – with goals from Horswill and Tueart. A crowd of 51,872 packed into Roker Park for the replay and saw Sunderland really turn on the style with a 3-1 win, thanks to two goals from Billy Hughes and a thunderous shot from Vic Halom which was surely a contender for goal of the season. In the quarter finals, Sunderland were paired with Second Division Luton Town at Roker Park. It was the only occasion that Sunderland were drawn against opposition from the same division as themselves during the 1972-1973 F.A. Cup run. In front of 53,151 screaming fans, most of them red and white, Dave Watson opened the scoring in the second half and Roker Park erupted. Tension took a grip on the game as Luton Town surged forward in search of the equaliser but the Sunderland defence held magnificently and when the second Sunderland goal arrived, again from a defender, this time courtesy of Ron Guthrie, the club were through to the semi finals for the first time since 1956. At the time, Arsenal were challenging for the league and cup double and when Sunderland's name came out of the bag with that of the Gunners few people outside of the North East would have bet against the North London team. The venue was Hillsborough and the result Arsenal 1 Sunderland 2 was the stuff that fairytales are made of. With Sunderland's "H Force", Halom and Hughes, on the rampage for the full ninety minutes, the Arsenal defence was run ragged. Halom and Hughes netted a goal apiece and although George pulled one back for the Gunners, anything other than a win for Sunderland would have been a traversty of justice. With a place at Wembley secured, cup fever swept to every corner of Wearside. Industry boomed, the clubs and pubs were buzzing with football talk, a sense of pride was restored to the town as the entire Sunderland population anticipated a Wembley victory against Leeds United. Come the big day, as the two teams strode out of the Wembley tunnel the noise was unbelievable. Leeds United could have been forgiven for thinking that their supporters had stayed in Yorkshire as red and white scarves appeared to fill all areas of the ground. The details of the actual game are well documented in the annals of football history. A goal from Ian Porterfield at 3.32pm and a breathtaking double save by Jimmy Montgomery midway through the second half brought the cup back to Roker Park for the first time in thirty six years.

**Incoming players included:**
Ray Ellison, Ron Guthrie, Vic Halom, John Hughes, David Young.

**Outgoing players included:**
Gordon Harris, Martin Harvey, John Hughes, Cecil Irwin, Paddy Lowery, Fred McIver, Colin Symm.

**Sunderland's league record read:**

| P | W | D | L | F | A | Pts | Position |
|---|---|---|---|---|---|-----|----------|
| 42 | 17 | 12 | 13 | 59 | 49 | 46 | 6th |

League appearances (with F.A. Cup and League Cup appearances in brackets): Ashurst 11 (1), Bolton 9 (2), Chambers 11, Coleman 17 (1), Ellison 2, Guthrie 15 (7), Halom 15 (5), Horswill 39 (8), Hughes J 1, Hughes W 29 (9), Kerr 41 (10), Lathan 20 (2), Malone 41 (10), McGiven 14 (2), Montgomery 41 (10), Pitt 21 (7), Porterfield 41 (10), Swinburne 1, Tones 2 (2), Tueart 41 (10), Watson 37 (10), Young 10 (2).

Average home attendance: 25,753

*A victorious Bobby Kerr holds the F.A. Cup following Sunderland's 1-0 defeat of Leeds United at Wembley.*

Total attendance during F.A. Cup games: 413,382

*Suprisingly, Argus refused to allow Sunderland's F.A. Cup success go to his head when he wrote in the "Roker Reflections" page of the Sunderland Football Echo. "The magnificent achievement in reaching Wembley stands on its own. No frills are needed to heighten the sense of pride which this has brought for everyone with a Sunderland interest at heart. This applies particularly to Mr. Stokoe and his players as well as to the directors and staff for the support which they have given. Yet it would be wrong to write this season into the record books as the one in which Sunderland won the F.A. Cup for only the second time in their history and to overlook the tremendous strides which have been taken at the same time in putting together a pattern of play which equips them better to tackle what must always be their major target – a return to the First Division at the earliest possible moment."*

# THEY'VE DONE IT!

This was the vital first goal which came after 31 minutes.   The man who scored was Ian Porterfield.

# Porterfield the hero in glorious Wembley victory

**CUP FINAL SPECIAL**

## SUNDERLAND - - - - - - 1   LEEDS UNITED - - - - - 0

SUNDERLAND'S proudest moment in 36 years arrived at Wembley this afternoon when they took on the might of Leeds United, one of British soccer's success sides over the last ten years, in the final of the F.A. Cup.

They carried with them their own vociferous supporters and a wealth of encouragement and sympathy from the vast majority of the 100,000 gathered in the stadium for this big occasion.

Heavy rain throughout the morning threatened to provide unpleasant conditions, but this stopped during the team's 70-minute drive to the stadium and when Frankie Vaughan climbed on the rostrum to lead the crowd in singing, the sun finally broke through.

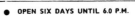

### BY ARGUS

When the teams walked out for presentations to the Duke of Kent, Leeds United manager Don Revie headed the Leeds procession wearing a lounge suit, but Sunderland manager Bob Stokoe was track-suited in the familiar red and white.

The break in the weather was not prolonged, however, and during the presentation the rain started again.

## Won toss

Kerr won the toss for Sunderland and elected to defend the end which had the Leeds supporters massed behind them.

A misplaced pass by Hunter right from the start was collec-

ted by Tueart, who had a shot charged down and when Horswill and Kerr tried to follow up, they both fell down on the slippery turf. Then Jones moved on the left, and was tackled firs by Watson and then Malone. He still managed to get the ball in the middle, where Clarke was brought down by Pitt to provide the first free-kick of the game.

Bremner moved it square for Lorimer, whose well-hit drive travelled wide, with Jones just failing to make contact.

When Leeds tried to move from a throw-in, Kerr inter-

cepted a crossfield pass and then left the ball to Hughes, who was brought down by Cherry.

The first trial of strength between Malone and Gray ended in the Sunderland player's favour, but when he tried to move down the wing Cherry's challenge sent the ball out of play.

In the next minutes Giles gave the ball away from a deep position and the chance was created for Tueart to go at the Leeds defence.

## Pushed down

Sunderland were in difficulties when Gray moved the ball inside to Giles, whose accurate crossfield pass was headed on by Reaney and lifted into the middle, where Montgomery could only push the ball down and the clearance was completed by Horswill.

A Bremner foul on Porterfield gave Sunderland a free kick just inside the Sunderland half, but Halom was unable to reach Malone's kick and the ball travelled on to Harvey.

Hughes was back to lend a hand in defence when Leeds tried again and he was obstructed by Jones when he

tried to bring the ball out.

Sunderland were in with a chance when Halom picked up a through-ball and sent Porterfield away on the left.

From Porterfield's centre Hughes got in a shot which lifted over the bar.

Then Leeds were up again and Giles and then Clarke had shots beaten down. Hunter went right through and though Kerr managed to get ahead, Hunter still reached the ball to send his shot behind the goal.

## Booked

Sunderland's hopes boomed when a left wing attack started from a throw-in with the ball sent back to Guthrie, and Hors-
(Continued in Back Page)

### THE TEAMS

SUNDERLAND — Montgomery; Malone, Guthrie, Horswill, Watson, Pitt, Kerr (capt.), Hughes, Halom, Porterfield, Tueart. Sub: Young.

LEEDS UNITED—Harvey, Reaney, Cherry, Bremner (capt.), Madeley, Hunter, Lorimer, Clarke, Jones, Giles, E. Gray. Sub: Yorath.

Referee: Mr Ken Burns (Stourbridge).

### IN THE PINK

WE'RE in the pink today. The Sports Edition of the Echo celebrates Sunderland's victory at Wembley by printing once again on pink paper.

*Sunderland 1 Leeds United 0. The F.A. Cup returned to Roker Park on 5th May 1973.*

## SUNDERLAND 1    LEEDS UNITED 0

Bobby Kerr won the toss for Sunderland and decided to defend the end which had been reserved for the Leeds fans.

An early misplaced pass by Hunter was picked up by Tueart whose shot was charged down. When a ball from Giles was crossed into the middle for Clarke, Pitt quickly sensed the danger and his challenge on the Leeds man, produced the first free kick of the game. Bremner took the kick from which Lorimer hit a shot which travelled wide. Sunderland's tenacious play was giving untold problems to the Leeds defence and an early feature of the game was the battle between Malone and Gray with the Sunderland player enjoying the better of the exchanges. Leeds were giving the ball away too regularly for the comfort of their supporters and on one occasion a misplaced pass from Giles was picked up by Tueart who raced towards the Leeds goal. It was not all Sunderland however and when Gray moved the ball inside to Giles a superb pass was headed on by Reaney and lifted into the middle where Montgomery was at full stretch to push the ball down for Horswill to clear the danger. After a Billy Hughes shot lifted over the bar, Sunderland had a great chance to open the scoring from an attack down the left hand side. Guthrie picked up a throw-in and when the ball broke to a well positioned Horswill he had the time and space to hit a right foot shot which travelled only inches wide. When Leeds won a free kick, a centre from Giles set up Clarke who was denied a shot on goal by a timely tackle by Watson. Hughes and Tueart were giving the Leeds defence all sorts of problems with their non stop running and it came as no surprise when Sunderland took the lead in the 31st minute. Kerr broke on the right and when he drove the ball into the middle, Harvey turned it over the bar for a corner. Hughes took the left wing corner and when it was pulled down in the middle, Porterfield controlled it beautifully before crashing a fierce shot into the net. When Tueart and Hughes worked a one-two, Hughes broke away from Cherry and crossed the ball into the middle for Halom but Harvey just got there first to clear the ball and when Horswill followed up he was upended on the line by Giles. The first half ended with a Leeds attack with Clarke gaining possession in the penalty area but, once again, Watson was in total command and prevented a clean shot.

Sunderland resumed their attacking play in the second half and had the best of the early exchanges. Watson and Pitt were towers of strength in defence although there was an anxious moment when Bremner picked up a ball just outside the penalty area and fired a strong shot which Montgomery failed to hold and Malone pushed behind for a corner. In the 65th minute, Montgomery made a fabulous double save from Jones and Cherry as Leeds suddenly started to look threatening. As Leeds pushed forward, gaps appeared at the back and Sunderland almost took advantage when a quick break with Halom, Horswill and Tueart set up a three against three situation. Shortly after Yorath came on for Gray he hit a low drive from the right which produced an excellent save from Montgomery. Seconds later, Kerr sent Horswill away but his shot was deflected for a corner. Tueart had a great chance to increase Sunderland's lead but Madeley defended well. Two minutes from time Kerr and Tueart opened up the Leeds defence when they presented a good chance for Halom but the Leeds keeper came to the rescue. However there was to be no way back for Leeds and the F.A. Cup deservedly came to Roker Park.

**Sunderland:** Montgomery, Malone, Guthrie, Horswill, Watson, Pitt, Kerr, Hughes, Halom, Porterfield, Tueart.

**Leeds United:** Harvey, Reaney, Cherry, Bremner, Madeley, Hunter, Lorimer, Clarke, Jones, Giles, Gray (Yorath).

"Wearsiders Take Over The Capital" proclaimed The Sunderland Echo in its 5th May 1973 edition. From early morning, the capital was aglow with red and white favours and emblems of all descriptions. Londoners - used to cup finals and other big event invasions - said they hadn't seen such enthusiasm for years.

The first of fourteen trains from Sunderland left just after 3.00am and as each of the trains departed cheering supporters hung out of the carriage windows. In all, 7,000 fans left Sunderland by train.

In Park Lane, the biggest-ever fleet of coaches run by United and Northern picked up hundreds of supporters shortly after midnight and the scene was described as "absolute chaos" by one observer. In all, sixty coaches were laid on to cope with demand.

Two Viscount charter planes left Newcastle Airport and another one took off from Teeside.

The town's taxi drivers said the scene was just like New Year's Eve with parties all over the town. "We couldn't get near the railway station for crowds. I've never seen anything like it in my life," said one driver.

The following day saw many of town's shops close for business at lunch time and come 3.00pm Market Square was absolutely deserted. Two hours later, the town erupted to the sound of car horns and people singing and dancing in the streets. Sunderland had done it! Against all the odds the Rokermen had defeated red hot favourites Leeds United and the cup was on its way to Wearside.

The team's homecoming exceeded all expectations. Well over 500,000 people lined the route as the team travelled by open top coach from Carrville in Durham into Sunderland via the Board Inn at Herrington and then along Durham Road into Holmeside, Fawcett Street, North Bridge Street and finally to Roker Park.

It was a carnival atmosphere all the way in one of the most emotionally charged settings ever witnessed in Sunderland.

# 1973-1974

Having won the F.A. Cup against all the odds during the previous season, Sunderland kicked off the 1973-1974 campaign with the single-minded aim of regaining their First Division status.

By coincidence, the first home game of the season brought Orient to Roker Park for the second successive season. It was a sign of Sunderland's new found status that a crowd of 28,211 turned up for the game compared with 12,658 for the corresponding fixture during the previous season. Although early results were disappointing with just four wins in their first ten league games, attendances remained fairly constant at just beneath thirty thousand and optimism remained undiminished.

Sunderland suffered their first set back of the season when Ritchie Pitt sustained a knee injury in the home game with Luton Town during September. The injury was more serious than at first thought and that game was to be Pitt's last for Sunderland. David Young, Jackie Ashurst and Rod Belfitt all had spells wearing the number six shirt during the course of the season with nothing more than moderate success. The team's composure was upset when Tueart, Horswill and Hughes submitted mid season transfer requests; the first two named players eventually leaving for Manchester City. A slump in form at the turn of the year which saw the team take just two points from seven games sent attendances spiralling beneath 20,000 for the first time in almost a year. Optimism was fading fast and the automatic promotion which many supporters had taken for granted at the start of the season was becoming a forlorn hope. The cup winning team had been rocked by injury and transfer requests and the team which concluded the league programme at Luton Town on 1st May 1974 showed three changes from the side which had triumphed at Wembley twelve months earlier.

An end of season placing of sixth in the Second Division was five places lower than most supporters would have predicted at the start of the campaign.

With three major cup trophies to compete for as well as promotion, Sunderland's resources were stretched to the limit. The team progressed to the second round of the European Cup Winners Cup following a 3-0 aggregate win over Hungarian team Vasas Budapest but lost out by an aggregate 3-2 to Sporting Lisbon of Portugal. The games failed to excite Roker supporters with disappointing attendances of 22,762 and 31,568 respectively.

It was a different story in the League Cup where Sunderland re-captured some of the excitement of the previous season's F.A. Cup exploits. A fine 2-2 draw against Derby County at the Baseball Ground, thanks to two goals from John Lathan, brought the top First Division team to Roker Park where 38,975 fans witnessed a thrilling 1-1 draw with a goal from Dennis Tueart. Rather than stage the second replay at a neutral ground, both clubs agreed to spin a coin for the choice of ground for the third match. Roker Park was chosen and the game produced one of Sunderland's best ever perforamnces with a Vic Halom hat trick paving the way for a convincing 3-0 victory. The next round brought mighty Liverpool to Roker Park but unfortunately a spirited performance by Sunderland could not prevent a 2-0 defeat.

Sunderland's surrender of the F.A. Cup to Second Division Carlisle United in their promotion season was something of an anticlimax but many felt that it left the way open for Bob Stokoe to concentrate on the main priority — promotion.

**Incoming players included:**
Rod Belfitt, Tim Gilbert, Danny Hegan, Dennis Longhorn, Peter Stronach, Tony Towers

**Outgoing players included:**
Keith Coleman, Brian Chambers, Derek Forster, Mick Horswill, John Lathan, Mick McGiven, John Tones, Dennis Tueart

**Sunderland's league record read:**

| P | W | D | L | F | A | Pts | Position |
|---|---|---|---|---|---|-----|----------|
| 42 | 19 | 9 | 14 | 58 | 44 | 47 | 6th |

League appearances (with F.A. Cup, League Cup and European Cup Winners Cup appearances in brackets) Ashurst 15 (2), Belfitt 30 (2), Bolton 26 (7), Guthrie 17 (3), Halom 38 (10), Hamilton 1, Hegan 3, Horswill 22 (9), Hughes 33 (8), Kerr 41 (10), Lathan 2 (1), Longhorn 12 (10), Malone 42, McGiven 5, Mitchell 1, Montgomery 41 (10), Pitt 4 (1), Porterfield 40 (10), Swinburne 1, Towers 8, Tueart 26 (9), Watson 41 (10), Young 13 (8)

Average home attendance: 26,164

This figure also included the European Cup Winners Cup

*Vic Halom was one of Bob Stokoe's first signings when he took over the manager's job at Roker Park.*

*There could have been few Sunderland supporters who did not echo the end of season summary by Argus when he wrote, "The Second Division is no place for a club like Sunderland with facilities, traditions and a following which is not bettered by any club in the land. Their place is among the elite. But they have no rights in the matter," continued Argus. "They are not 'entitled' to be there. Nor do they 'belong' or 'deserve' to be there. They are in the Second Division because of what they have been and getting back into the First Division is a matter of being good enough."*

## VASAS (Budapest) 0    SUNDERLAND 2

The game's first quarter saw Vasas give a demonstration of brilliant attacking play as they swept forward with some fine passing movements. The first real chance of the game arrived when an in-swinging ball from Sipocz crashed against a post. Tueart and Hughes both came close before Halom tested goalkeeper Meszaros who made a good save. As the half came to a close, Montgomery was in action following a quick break down the right wing by Torok who centred for Muller.

Three good chances fell to Vasas early in the second half. First Vidate bent a free kick from 25 yards which Montgomery did well to hold. The same player then thundered an angle shot from the right which struck the far post. There was an anxious moment when Vasas were awarded an indirect free kick from inside the Sunderland penalty area and when the ball was tapped to Varadi, his fierce shot went just wide. Sunderland won a free kick when Tueart was brought down by Toth. Malone's resulting free kick found the advancing Meszaros in no man's land as Hughes headed into an empty net. In the 89th minute Porterfield found Tueart who beat two men on the turn before holding off a third and sliding the ball wide of Meszaros for a brilliant solo goal.

**Vasas:** Mesaros, Torok, Fabian, Karntor, Lakinger (Gass), Vidate, Muller, Toth, Varadi, Kovacs, Sipocz.

**Sunderland:** Montgomery, Malone, Guthrie, Horswill, Watson, Pitt, Kerr, Hughes, Halom (Young), Porterfield, Tueart.

# 1974-1975

Sunderland entered the new year with just four defeats in twenty four games and their promotion prospects looked good.

Bryan Robson's transfer from West Ham United was completed for a then club record fee of £145,000 while Bobby Moncur arrived from Newcastle United. Moncur's experience tightened the defence to the extent that only eight goals were conceded all season at Roker Park; thus creating a club record while the thirty five goals conceded in total was the lowest since 1900-1901 season.

The club suffered a sickening blow when Ian Porterfield was badly injured in a motoring accident and was to play no further part in first team action that season. Porterfield's prolonged absence and consistently good performances by promotion rivals Manchester United and Aston Villa were to deny Sunderland that elusive promotion place with Norwich City nosing ahead of Bob Stokoe's men to claim the third promotion spot.

With Sunderland missing out on promotion by three points in 1973-1974 season and just two points in the current campaign, many supporters likened the situation to seasons 1961-1962 and 1962-1963 when promotion was whisked away at the final hurdles.

There was little joy to be gleaned from either domestic cup competition with instant dismissal from the League Cup by Preston North End and defeat by Middlesbrough in the fourth round of the F.A. Cup.

**Incoming players included:**
Tom Finney, Mick Henderson, Bobby Moncur, Bryan Robson

**Outgoing players included:**
Rod Belfitt, Ray Ellison, Maurice Hepworth, Danny Hegan, David Young

*Jeff Clark who came to Sunderland from Manchester City in June 1975.*

**Sunderland's league record read:**

| P | W | D | L | F | A | Pts | Position |
|---|---|---|---|---|---|-----|----------|
| 42 | 19 | 13 | 10 | 65 | 35 | 51 | 4th |

League appearances (with F.A. Cup and League Cup appearances in brackets)
Ashurst 3 (1), Belfitt 6, Bolton 20 (2), Finney 1 (1), Guthrie 34 (1), Halom 36 (3), Hughes 42 (3), Kerr 42 (3), Longhorn 15 (2), Malone 42 (3), Moncur 42 (3), Montgomery 40 (2), Porterfield 14, Robson 42 (3), Swinburne 2 (1), Towers 41 (2), Watson 40 (3)

Average home attendance: 30,116

*Argus looked back on a season of what might have been when he wrote, "From the assured position of only a few short months ago, Sunderland approached the final dramatic stages of the promotion race overwhelmed by uncertainty and in the race of rank outsiders. The time has come for positive thinking . . . to the question of whether the team which failed to win promotion this season is good enough to try again, the answer has to be in the negative. For two seasons, when at their best, the team looked ready made for the First Division. But for two seasons they have been pulled back by their own shortcomings which has too often taken the form of poor application and a lack of professionalism. To reach the promotion target, Sunderland require a team of hungry fighters ... and to stay hungry. There have been too many dark grey patches of form which have been frequent reminders of the occasions when the appetite was less than adequate."*

# Echo
## SUNDERLAND

No. 32,511 (103rd Year)  SATURDAY, APRIL 24, 1976  6p

# They're the champions

## Today's results

# ROKER CLINCH TITLE IN STYLE

Bryan Robson powers home a left foot shot despite the close at tention of a Pompey defender in this afternoon's match at Roker Park.

### DIVISION I

Aston Villa 2 Middlesbro 1
(Half-time: 1—1)
Burnley ... 1 Coventry .. 3
(Half-time: 1—0)
Everton ... 2 West Ham 0
(Half-time: 2—0)
Ipswich .. 2 Derby ... 6
(Half-time: 2—3)
Leicester . 2 Man. Utd. 1
(Half-time: 1—0)
Man.. City 3 Arsenal ... 1
(Half-time: 1—1)
QPR ... 2 Leeds Utd 0
(Half-time: 1—0)
Stoke ... 0 Norwich ... 2
(Half-time: 0—0)
Tottenham 0 Newcastle 3
(Half-time: 0—0)

| | P | W | D | L | F | A | Pt |
|---|---|---|---|---|---|---|---|
| Q P R | 42 | 24 | 11 | 7 | 67 | 33 | 59 |
| Liverpool | 42 | 22 | 14 | 5 | 63 | 30 | 58 |
| Man. Utd. | 41 | 22 | 10 | 9 | 66 | 42 | 54 |
| Derby | 41 | 21 | 10 | 10 | 75 | 58 | 53 |
| Leeds Utd. | 42 | 21 | 9 | 12 | 65 | 46 | 51 |
| Ipswich | 42 | 16 | 14 | 12 | 54 | 48 | 46 |
| Leicester | 42 | 13 | 19 | 10 | 48 | 51 | 45 |
| Man. City | 41 | 16 | 11 | 14 | 64 | 44 | 43 |
| Tottenham | 42 | 13 | 16 | 13 | 63 | 63 | 43 |
| Norwich | 42 | 16 | 10 | 16 | 58 | 58 | 42 |
| Everton | 42 | 15 | 12 | 15 | 60 | 66 | 42 |
| Stoke City | 42 | 15 | 11 | 16 | 48 | 50 | 41 |
| Middlesbrough | 42 | 15 | 10 | 17 | 46 | 45 | 40 |
| Coventry | 42 | 13 | 14 | 15 | 47 | 57 | 40 |
| Aston Villa | 42 | 11 | 17 | 14 | 51 | 59 | 39 |
| Newcastle | 42 | 15 | 9 | 18 | 71 | 62 | 39 |
| West Ham | 42 | 13 | 10 | 19 | 47 | 53 | 36 |
| Birmingham | 41 | 13 | 6 | 22 | 56 | 74 | 32 |
| Wolves | 41 | 10 | 10 | 21 | 50 | 66 | 30 |
| Burnley | 42 | 9 | 10 | 23 | 43 | 66 | 28 |
| Sheffield Utd. | 41 | 6 | 9 | 26 | 32 | 81 | 21 |

### DIVISION III

Brighton .. 1 Sheff Wed.1
(Half-time: 0—1)
Grimsby .. 2 Gillingham 1
(Half-time: 1—1)
Halifax ... 1 Aldershot 0
(Half-time: 1—1)
Hereford \ 3 Rotherham 2
(Half-time: 1—1)
Mansfield 0 Colchester 0
(Half-time: 0—0)
Peterboro' 3 Shr'wsb'ry 2
(Half-time: 0—1)
Preston .. 3 Port Vale . 0
(Half-time: 1—0)
Swindon . 5 Walsall ... 1
(Half-time: 2—1)

| | P | W | D | L | F | A | Pt |
|---|---|---|---|---|---|---|---|
| Hereford | 45 | 25 | 11 | 9 | 83 | 54 | 61 |
| Millwall | 46 | 20 | 19 | 10 | 54 | 43 | 56 |
| Cardiff | 46 | 21 | 13 | 11 | 68 | 48 | 55 |
| Brighton | 44 | 21 | 13 | 10 | 75 | 48 | 55 |
| Crystal Plce | 44 | 18 | 16 | 10 | 60 | 44 | 52 |
| Wrexham | 44 | 20 | 10 | 14 | 82 | 61 | 50 |
| Walsall | 46 | 18 | 14 | 14 | 74 | 61 | 50 |
| Shrewsbury | 46 | 19 | 10 | 17 | 61 | 59 | 48 |
| Peterborough | 46 | 15 | 18 | 13 | 63 | 63 | 48 |
| Preston | 45 | 19 | 10 | 16 | 61 | 59 | 48 |
| Mansfield | 46 | 16 | 15 | 15 | 58 | 52 | 47 |
| Port Vale | 46 | 15 | 16 | 15 | 55 | 54 | 46 |
| Gillingham | 46 | 12 | 19 | 15 | 56 | 65 | 43 |
| Rotherham | 44 | 15 | 12 | 19 | 56 | 65 | 42 |
| Bury | 44 | 13 | 16 | 15 | 50 | 45 | 42 |
| Chesterfield | 45 | 17 | 8 | 20 | 69 | 69 | 42 |
| Grimsby | 45 | 15 | 10 | 21 | 62 | 74 | 40 |
| Chester | 44 | 14 | 12 | 18 | 41 | 60 | 40 |
| Aldershot | 46 | 13 | 14 | 18 | 16 | 75 | 69 | 40 |
| Swindon | 46 | 16 | 7 | 22 | 60 | 73 | 38 |
| Sheffield W | 45 | 11 | 16 | 18 | 46 | 56 | 38 |
| Colchester | 46 | 11 | 12 | 23 | 40 | 64 | 37 |
| Southend | 45 | 11 | 13 | 20 | 62 | 71 | 36 |
| Halifax | 45 | 11 | 12 | 22 | 40 | 60 | 34 |

### SCOTTISH DIV. II

Brechin ... 1 Berwick R 0
(Half-time: 1—0)
Stranraer .. 1 Stirling Alb 0
(Half-time: 0—0)

### SCOTTISH PREMIER DIVISION

| | P | W | D | L | F | A | Pt |
|---|---|---|---|---|---|---|---|
| Rangers | 33 | 22 | 6 | 5 | 56 | 24 | 50 |
| Celtic | 33 | 20 | 5 | 7 | 66 | 38 | 45 |
| Hibernian | 34 | 18 | 7 | 9 | 55 | 38 | 43 |
| Motherwell | 33 | 16 | 7 | 10 | 55 | 45 | 39 |
| Aberdeen | 35 | 10 | 10 | 15 | 48 | 50 | 30 |
| Dundee Utd | 33 | 11 | 8 | 14 | 37 | 45 | 30 |
| Hearts | 33 | 11 | 6 | 16 | 34 | 44 | 28 |
| Ayr | 33 | 11 | 7 | 15 | 42 | 59 | 29 |
| Dundee | 34 | 10 | 9 | 15 | 47 | 61 | 29 |
| St Johnstone | 34 | 3 | 9 | 22 | 29 | 78 | 10 |

Today's games not included.

### DIVISION II

Bristol C. 1 Notts Co .. 2
(Half-time: 0—1)
Carlisle .. 2 Plymouth . 0
(Half-time: 1—0)
Charlton .. 0 Bolton ... 4
(Half-time: 0—1)
Fulham ... 1 Blackburn 1
(Half-time: 0—1)
Luton T .. 3 Blackpool 0
(Half-time: 1—0)
Nottm For. 3 Bristol R. 0
(Half-time: 1—0)
Oldham A 0 WBA ... 1
(Half-time: 0—0)
Orient ... 2 Oxford Utd 1
(Half-time: 1—0)
S'thampton 1 Hull City . 0
(Half-time: 1—0)
Sunderland 2 Portsm'th . 0
(Half-time: 2—0)
York City 2 Chelsea .. 2
(Half-time: 1—0)

| | P | W | D | L | F | A | Pt |
|---|---|---|---|---|---|---|---|
| Sunderland | 42 | 24 | 8 | 10 | 67 | 36 | 56 |
| Bristol City | 42 | 19 | 15 | 8 | 59 | 35 | 53 |
| West Brom | 42 | 20 | 13 | 9 | 50 | 33 | 53 |
| Bolton | 41 | 19 | 12 | 10 | 61 | 37 | 50 |
| Southampton | 42 | 21 | 7 | 14 | 66 | 50 | 49 |
| Luton | 42 | 19 | 10 | 13 | 61 | 51 | 48 |
| Notts County | 41 | 18 | 12 | 12 | 58 | 41 | 47 |
| Nottm For. | 42 | 17 | 12 | 13 | 55 | 40 | 46 |
| Charlton | 42 | 15 | 12 | 15 | 61 | 72 | 42 |
| Blackpool | 42 | 14 | 14 | 14 | 40 | 49 | 42 |
| Chelsea | 42 | 12 | 16 | 14 | 53 | 54 | 40 |
| Fulham | 42 | 13 | 14 | 15 | 45 | 47 | 40 |
| Orient | 41 | 13 | 14 | 14 | 37 | 32 | 39 |
| Hull City | 42 | 14 | 11 | 17 | 45 | 49 | 39 |
| Blackburn | 42 | 12 | 14 | 16 | 45 | 50 | 38 |
| Plymouth | 42 | 13 | 12 | 17 | 48 | 54 | 38 |
| Bristol R. | 41 | 11 | 16 | 14 | 37 | 47 | 38 |
| Oldham | 42 | 13 | 12 | 17 | 57 | 68 | 38 |
| Carlisle | 442 | 12 | 13 | 17 | 45 | 59 | 37 |
| Oxford | 42 | 11 | 12 | 19 | 39 | 59 | 34 |
| York City | 42 | 10 | 8 | 24 | 39 | 71 | 28 |
| Portsmouth | 42 | 9 | 7 | 26 | 32 | 61 | 25 |

### DIVISION IV

Barnsley v Southport
(Half-time: 1—0)
Late kick-off—Result in Stop Press
Bradford C 1 Cambridge 2
(Half-time: 1—0)
Darlington 2 Bourn'm'th 0
(Half-time: 1—0)
Hartlepool 1 Brentford . 0
(Half-time: 1—0)
Hud'rsfield 1 Watford .. 0
(Half-time: 0—0)
Newport . 2 Work'ngt'n 3
(Half-time: 1—0)
Reading .. 3 Crewe ... 1
(Half-time: 1—0)
Torquay .. 2 Lincoln C. 2
(Half-time: 1—0)

| | P | W | D | L | F | A | Pt |
|---|---|---|---|---|---|---|---|
| Lincoln | 45 | 32 | 9 | 4 | 110 | 38 | 73 |
| Northampton | 46 | 24 | 12 | 10 | 87 | 40 | 60 |
| Reading | 46 | 24 | 10 | 12 | 70 | 51 | 60 |
| Tranmere | 46 | 24 | 9 | 12 | 86 | 52 | 57 |
| Huddersfield | 45 | 20 | 13 | 11 | 56 | 41 | 56 |
| Bournemouth | 46 | 20 | 11 | 14 | 56 | 47 | 51 |
| Torquay | 46 | 17 | 14 | 15 | 64 | 63 | 50 |
| Watford | 46 | 18 | 12 | 16 | 62 | 62 | 50 |
| Exeter | 46 | 18 | 14 | 14 | 56 | 47 | 50 |
| Doncaster | 46 | 19 | 11 | 16 | 75 | 69 | 49 |
| Swansea | 46 | 16 | 13 | 15 | 63 | 54 | 45 |
| Cambridge | 46 | 14 | 15 | 17 | 58 | 62 | 43 |
| Barnsley | 45 | 13 | 16 | 16 | 50 | 48 | 42 |
| Hartlepool | 46 | 16 | 10 | 20 | 62 | 78 | 42 |
| Rochdale | 46 | 12 | 18 | 16 | 40 | 64 | 42 |
| Crewe | 46 | 13 | 15 | 18 | 51 | 75 | 41 |
| Brentford | 46 | 14 | 12 | 20 | 56 | 59 | 40 |
| Scunthorpe | 46 | 14 | 10 | 22 | 50 | 59 | 38 |
| Stockport | 46 | 13 | 12 | 21 | 43 | 76 | 38 |
| Darlington | 45 | 14 | 9 | 22 | 47 | 56 | 37 |
| Bradford | 43 | 11 | 15 | 17 | 57 | 82 | 37 |
| Newport | 45 | 13 | 9 | 23 | 50 | 67 | 35 |
| Southport | 45 | 8 | 10 | 27 | 44 | 76 | 26 |
| Workington | 46 | 7 | 7 | 32 | 30 | 87 | 21 |

### SCOTTISH SPRING CUP

Airdrie ... 5 Hamilton 2
(Half-time: 2—0)
East Fife . 1 Clydebank 0
(Half-time: 1—0)
Falkirk ... 1 Dumbarton 2
(Half-time: 1—0)
St Mirren . 0 Morton ... 1
(Half-time: 0—0)

### F.A. TROPHY — FINAL

Scarboro' 2 Stafford .. 2
(Half-time: 0—0)

### SCOTTISH PREMIER LEAGUE

Aberdeen 3 Hibernian . 0
(Half-time: 1—0)
Celtic ... 1 Ayr U. ... 2
(Half-time: 1—0)
Dundee U 0 Rangers .. 1
(Half-time: 0—1)
Hearts ... 1 St J'hnst'n 0
(Half-time: 1—0)
Motherwell 1 Dundee ... 1
(Half-time: 0—1)

## Sunderland - - - 2
## Portsmouth - - - 0

SUNDERLAND go back to the First Division as champions of the Second and a 40,515 Roker Park crowd cheered them all the way as they made sure of the title with a decisive win over Portsmouth at Roker Park this afternoon.

The first goal of the season by Bolton set them on their way and there was never any doubt afterwards that they were going to make it.

The red and white clad supporters broke the rule which they have observed throughout the season by streaming onto the pitch as the game ended to start the rounds of celebrations.

Swinburne continued in goal for Sunderland in the absence of Montgomery, but both Malone and Kerr were able to return.

Greenwood was named as substitute with Hughes holding the No. 11 position.

Portsmouth had to make a change at No. 5 with regular centre half Paul Cahill starting a two-game suspension. His place was taken by Paul Went who has just resumed after being out for two months with an ankle injury.

### BY ARGUS

Went won the toss for Portsmouth and Sunderland started the game attacking the Fulwell End.

Went intercepted to prevent Bolton from going clear in an overlap on the left and then Holden carried a little luck in being able to keep a right wing attack going before the ball was turned over for a throw-in on the right.

Kerr's throw was met by Ellis at the near post but his header failed to clear it and an overhead kick by Holden presented Hughes with a glorious chance but from a couple of yards he was unable to get a header on the target.

Hughes was caught offside when Kerr tried to reach him with a through ball, following an excellent cross by Train. Figgins dived out to grab the ball at Hugh's feet when Kerr sent a free-kick into the middle and then the Portsmouth goalkeeper was in action again, diving along his line to hold a 25-yard drive by Robson.

McGuinness won the ball against Bolton for Piper to make a centre but Swinburne left his line quickly to reach the ball well ahead of Kamara.

Handling by Hughes enabled Portsmouth to build up quickly from the free-kick with Earnes going away on the right only to drop his centre behind the goal.

Next Moncur opened up the Portsmouth defence but a good ball which was turned on for Robson who went wide on the left only to have his shot beaten down.

Swinburne picked up a tame long shot from Graham but when they came back again Moncur had to intervene after Graham had headed on a Went free kick.

### Swinburne tested

led from behind by Roberts on Hughes went down when tackled the left wing but there was no progress from Bolton's free kick and Portsmouth were quickly on going through the middle to the attack again with Roberts test Swinburne with a left-foot shot.

Holden moved away on the left from a Kerr pass to force
(Continued in Back Page)

### THE TEAMS

| SUNDERLAND | PORTSMOUTH |
|---|---|
| 1 Swinburne | 1 Figgins |
| 2 Malone | 2 Roberts |
| 3 Bolton | 3 Ellis |
| 4 Towers | 4 Kamara |
| 5 Ashurst | 5 Went |
| 6 Moncur | 6 Denyer |
| 7 Kerr | 7 Earnes |
| 8 Train | 8 Piper |
| 9 Holden | 9 Graham |
| 10 Robson | 10 Mellows |
| 11 Hughes | 11 McGuinness |
| Sub: Greenwood. | Sub. Wilson |

Referee: Mr R. Chadwick of Derwin.

*Sunderland were crowned Second Division champions in 1976 and returned to top flight football after a six year absence.*

# 1975-1976

During the close season, Dave Watson left the club for Manchester City in a deal which included centre half Jeff Clarke moving in the opposite direction. Another close season capture by Bob Stokoe was Mel Holden who arrived from Preston North End. Both signings were instant successes; Jeff Clarke quickly establishing an excellent defensive understanding with Bobby Moncur while Mel Holden soon hit the goals trail with Bryan Robson.

This was to be Sunderland's championship season and the statistics speak for themselves. The club won nineteen and drew two of their twenty one home games and so for the fifth time in their entire history played a full season undefeated at home. Goals came from all directions with no fewer than fifteen Sunderland players hitting the back of the net.

There were mixed fortunes in the cup competitions. Sunderland's interest in the League Cup was terminated in the first round when they were beaten 2-1 by Notts County at Meadow Lane. In the F.A. Cup, it looked for a while like 1973 re-visited. The third round produced a home tie with Oldham Athletic and a crowd of 29,226 saw goals from Holden and Robson dispose of the Lancashire side. A lone goal from Finney against Hull City in the next round set up a tricky fifth round tie at Stoke City. A magnificent defensive display in that game brought the Potteries side to Roker Park for the replay which Sunderland won 2-1 with Holden and Robson scoring the goals. A win at home against Malcolm Allison's Crystal Palace would have sent Sunderland through to the quarter finals and supporters hopes of another trip to Wembley soaring. However, despite Sunderland's unbeaten home record in the league, the Londoners won 1-0. Sunderland's magnificent support was emphasised by the fact that the four F.A. Cup games at Roker Park were watched by no fewer than 159,979 people.

Attendances at Roker Park were easily the highest in the division, beating the second highest by an aveage of 12,000.

**Incoming players included:**
Jeff Clarke, Mick Coady, Shaun Elliott, Tommy Gibb, Roy Greenwood, Mel Holden, Gary Rowell, Ray Train

**Outgoing players included:**
Ron Guthrie, Vic Halom, Jimmy Hamilton, Bobby Park, Ritchie Pitt, Dave Watson

**Sunderland's league record read:**

| P | W | D | L | F | A | Pts | Position |
|---|---|---|---|---|---|-----|----------|
| 42 | 24 | 8 | 10 | 67 | 36 | 56 | 1st |

League appearances (with F.A. Cup and League Cup appearances in brackets): Ashurst 20 (3), Bolton 34 (6), Clarke 31 (6), Finney 7 (5), Gibb 5, Greenwood 13, Halom 21 (2), Henderson 11 (1), Holden 31 (6), Hughes 14, Kerr 40 (6), Longhorn 6 (1), Malone 39 (5), Moncur 39 (6), Montgomery 38 (6), Porterfield 20 (1), Robson 40 (6), Rowell 3, Swinburne 4, Towers 34 (6), Train 12

Average home attendance: 32,661

*Tony Towers who joined the club from Manchester City in March 1974 in a deal which saw Mick Horswill travel in the opposite direction.*

"Penance Is Now Over" proclaimed Argus in the final edition of The Sunderland Football Echo of the 1975-1976 season. "Sunderland are back in the First Division again on the crest of a wave," said Argus. "Six years of punishment — or penance — in the wastes of the Second Divison are behind them now as the last piece of the expansion jigsaw falls into place. So much has been geared for precisely this moment that it can only come as an irritation for those who have worked hardest to find their successful challenge described as marking the end of their spell as the "poor relations" of North East football. Whatever else they may have been — and they have been many things in their time — they have never been poor relations in this area. The team which was good enough to win promotion is entitled to the chance of proving that it can make a go of it in the First Division. The same courtesy was never extended to the side which gained promotion in 1964 for they never played together again once the Second Division had been left behind."

# 1976-1977

Sunderland's resumption of life in the First Division got off to an indifferent start. There were four early season signings in Barry Siddall (from Bolton Wanderers), Bob Lee (from Leicester City), and Alan Foggon and Jim Holton (from Manchester United).

Sunderland failed to win any of their first ten league games and manager Bob Stokoe resigned after the home defeat by Aston Villa on 16th October. Ian McFarlane took charge of the team in a caretaker capacity until Jimmy Adamson was appointed as manager on 30th November. During his six weeks in charge, Mr. McFarlane sold Bryan Robson back to West Ham United, released Bobby Moncur to Carlisle United and took five points from seven league games.

Jimmy Adamson's first six weeks in charge were disastrous. Seven straight defeats, eleven goals conceded and none scored dumped Sunderland firmly at the bottom of the First Division. Sunderland had lost the two games immediately before Adamson's arrival and perhaps more significant was the fact that when the team took to the field to face Bristol City on 11th February 1977, Sunderland had failed to score since 23rd November 1976 when Billy Hughes found the net in a 3-1 defeat at Ipswich. Unusually, the home game against Bristol City was a Friday evening fixture and almost as unusual was the fact that Sunderland actually scored a goal. It was a Mel Holden effort in the Roker End and it was as if a cloud had lifted from Roker Park. Incredibly, the next three games, all at home, produced sixteen goals for Sunderland. The teams on the receiving end of Sunderland's goal scoring exploits were Middlesbrough (4-0), West Bromwich Albion (6-1) and West Ham United (6-0). Goal scorers were Bob Lee (5), Mel Holden (4), Gary Rowell (4) Bobby Kerr (1), Shaun Elliott (1) and Kevin Arnott (1).

The sensational impact of fielding Arnott, Elliott and Rowell suddenly made First Division survival a real possibility. Indeed, Sunderland went into the final game of the season at Everton having lost only two games since that sixteen goal blast and knowing that a draw could be good enough to save them from the drop. However, it wasn't to be as Sunderland lost 2-0 and were relegated, albeit in controversial circumstances. Fellow relegation candidates Coventry City and Bristol City started their game late and once the Sunderland result was broadcast around Highfield Road, both teams played out a goalless draw in the knowledge that one point was sufficient to guarantee their mutual survival.

In the League Cup, Sunderland beat Luton Town 3-1 and then took part in another marathon cup tie with Manchester United. Two 2-2 draws firstly at Old Trafford and then after extra time at Roker Park were followed by a 1-0 away defeat. Sunderland's inconsistent form in cup competitions re-surfaced with a defeat by Wrexham in the third round of the F.A. Cup.

**Incoming players included:**
Kevin Arnott, Alan Brown, Doug Collins, Mick Docherty, Alan Foggon, Jim Holton, Bob Lee, Barry Siddall, Colin Waldron

**Outgoing players included:**
Tom Finney, Tommy Gibb, Jim Holton, Dennis Longhorn, Bobby Moncur, Jimmy Montgomery, Bryan Robson, Ray Train

**Sunderland's league record read:**

| P | W | D | L | F | A | Pts | Position |
|---|---|---|---|---|---|-----|----------|
| 42 | 11 | 12 | 19 | 46 | 54 | 34 | 20th |

*Gary Rowell, one of Sunderland's most prolific goal scorers of recent years, joined the club from Seaham Juniors in 1975.*

League appearances (with F.A. Cup and League Cup appearances in brackets): Arnott 19, Ashurst 30 (4), Bolton 42 (6), Brown 5 (1), Clarke 27 (6), Coady 1, Collins 2, Docherty 20, Elliott 19 (1), Foggon 7 (2), Gibb 2, Greenwood 14 (2), Henderson 8 (1) Holden 24 (3), Holton 15 (4), Hughes 18 (5), Kerr 28 (4), Lee 32 (1), Longhorn 2, Malone 9 (3), Moncur 5 (1), Montgomery 6 (4), Robson 8 (4), Rowell 27 (3), Siddall 34 (2), Swinburne 2, Towers 25 (4), Train 19 (5), Waldron 12

Average home attendance: 31,843

"So that's it!", said Argus in the end of season Sunderland Football Echo. "The impossible dream is all over because it did not work out right in the end and Sunderland go back to the Second Division to start their rise to the top all over again. To finish one point short of a miraculous escape was nothing short of tragedy for the eager Sunderland players. Under the guidance of Jimmy Adamson and Dave Merrington, a fresh Sunderland image was created and as they climbed mountain after mountain from a ridiculously low start, it seemed that fate could not be cruel enough to snatch the due rewards of their efforts away from them at the last moment. In four magical months Adamson and Merrington have applied a set of values to the club which have brought fresh and young talent into harness to make an exciting team of tremendous potential. As one chapter closes, Sunderland are ready to start the next with a management team second to none and a young side which will come up fresh for next season bursting with ambition to fulfil itself. So from the impossible dream that failed, the scene will change to the grim reality of promotion fighting. It promises to be an exciting season and one to which fans will look with great confidence."

**Division 1 1976-1977** | **SUNDERLAND 6    WEST HAM UNITED 0**

Following emphatic home victories over Middlesbrough (4-0) and West Bromwich Albion (6-1), the crowd of 35,357 were hoping for another goal scoring blitz. They did not have to wait long as the enterprising Rowell won the ball on the left wing and whipped in a cross for Holden to beat Day for an early goal. Six minutes later, Arnott received a neat back-heeler and broke down the right wing before crossing the ball to a waiting Rowell to turn his shot wide of Day. West Ham were not in the game as an attacking force and they went further behind on the half hour when Day could only punch away a Kerr corner. When Waldron returned the ball into the middle, Holden rose to head the ball into the net and passed Day who was well off his line.

The second half saw Sunderland take full advantage of having the wind behind them as they continued to surge forward. Kerr intercepted a square ball by Lock on the 18 yard line to run home Sunderland's fourth goal on 53 minutes before going further ahead eleven minutes later. When a throw-in by Joe Bolton was played back to him by Lee, the ball ran loose for Rowell to hit a piledriver between Day and the near post. West Ham's agony was completed in the 85th minute when Bob Lee successfully played the offside trap as he accepted the ball from Docherty on the half-way line and raced through to beat the advancing Day.

**Sunderland:** Siddall, Docherty, Bolton, Arnott, Waldron, Ashurst, Kerr, Elliott, Holden, Lee, Rowell.

**West Ham United:** Day, Bonds, Lampard, Otulakowski, Green, Lock, Robson, Radford, Devonshire, Brooking, Jennings.

*Two players who clocked up almost four hundred post-war appearances between them. Jack Stelling and Len Duns played forty one and thirty three first team games respectively during 1946-1947 season.*

*Arthur Hudgell signed for Sunderland in 1947 and missed only six games between the 1947-1948 and 1950-1951 seasons. He played most of his games at left back although he did deputise for Jack Stelling at right back on occasions. Stelling and Hudgell were the regular Sunderland full backs at this time.*

*Tommy Reynolds was one of Sunderland's first post-war signings. He played most of his games in the number eleven shirt and was sold to Darlington in 1954.*

*Sunderland A.F.C.'s pre-season team photograph of 1948-1949. These were the golden days of football as a spectator sport and despite finishing in a moderate eighth position in the First Division, the average attendance at Roker Park was in excess of forty five thousand.*

*This photograph of Willie Fraser, Len Shackleton and Ted Purdon was taken in August 1956.*

*Colin Nelson was Sunderland's regular right back during the late fifties and early sixties. After playing 142 games for the club between 1958 and 1963, he eventually made way for Cecil Irwin during the 1963-1964 promotion season.*

*Sunderland's first team squad prior to the start of the 1951-1952 season.*

*Willie McPheat who made 72 appearances and scored 23 goals for Sunderland in the early sixties in action against Portsmouth at Roker Park on 21st January 1961.*

*Brian Clough leaves the field at Roker Park in 1962 following a 2-1 home win against Derby County.*

*Jack Hedley and Ray Daniel in action against Newcastle United at Roker Park on 19th December 1953. The game ended 1-1 with Stan Anderson scoring for Sunderland.*

*Ivor Broadis made his debut for Sunderland in 1948-1949 season. An England international.*

*The Sunderland team of 1961-1962.*

*Charlie Hurley, Ernie Taylor and Don Kichenbrand in 1959.*

*Nick Sharkey who scored five goals for Sunderland in a league game against Norwich City on 20th March 1963.*

*Harry Hooper in action at Roker Park during 1961-1962 season. Hooper was signed from Birmingham City for £18,000 at the start of 1960-1961 season. He made a total of eighty appearances for Sunderland and scored nineteen goals.*

Jim Baxter arrived at Roker Park from Glasgow Rangers in May 1965 when Sunderland manager Ian McColl paid £72,500 to the Scottish club for the international midfield player.

Sunderland manager Ian McColl and new signing Brian Heslop in discussion at Newcastle Airport. Heslop cost Sunderland £5,000 when he joined them from Carlisle United prior to the start of the 1967-1968 season.

Jimmy Montgomery's 623 first team appearances for his home town club span the period from 1962 to 1976 and is a club record which will not be beaten in the foreseeable future.

Scottish inernational Neil Martin played for Sunderland from November 1965 to February 1968.

Martin Harvey was one of many successes of Alan Brown's youth policy of the late fifties/early sixties. He was a one-club player whose career spanned 1959 1960 to 1971-1972 seasons and was capped by Northern Ireland on a regular basis.

One of Ian McColl's final decisions as Sunderland manager was to sign Gordon Harris from Burnley in January 1968. Following McColl's departure Harris was a regular member of the Alan Brown teams of the 1968-1969, 1969-1970 and 1970-1971 seasons. He is seen here during a training session with coach Billy Elliott and Ian Porterfield whose arrival at Roker Park preceeded that of Harris by just ten days. Porterfield stayed at the club until July 1977.

Alan Brown pictured on his return to Sunderland for his second stint as manager.

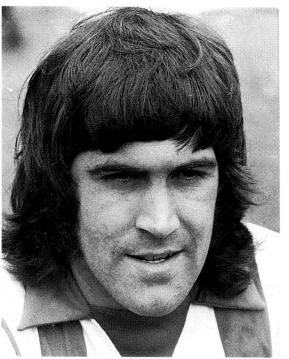

*Late sixties signing Colin Symm.*

*Billy Hughes joined Sunderland as a junior towards the end of 1965 and spent eleven seasons at the club during which time he scored 79 goals in 304 first time appearances. Four of those goals were scored in the 1973 F.A. Cup competition.*

*Dave Watson came to Sunderland from Rotherham United as a centre forward but was moved by caretaker manager Billy Elliott to the centre half position.*

*The Sunderland team take the field in the F.A. Cup Final at Wembley on 5th May 1973.*

*Bobby Kerr's 413 appearances for Sunderland ranks him in joint sixth position in the club's appearances table.*

*Roy Greenwood arrived at Roker Park from Hull City in a £140,000 deal on 8th January 1976. He was not an outstanding success and played only fifty games during his three year stay at the club.*

*The F.A. Cup winning team of 1973.*

*When Alan Durban signed Bryan Robson from Chelsea in July 1983 it was the player's third stint at Roker Park. Manager and player are seen here shortly after the signing. Both men are currently part of Peter Reid's backroom staff.*

*Ken Knighton and Frank Clark were appointed as the management duo prior to the start of the 1979-1980 season.*

*Frank Worthington joined Sunderland late in his career and is seen here making his debut for the club against Ipswich Town on 4th December 1982. He scored one goal that day but the team lost 3-2.*

*The Sunderland team of 1980-1981.*

*The Sunderland team of 1976-1977.*

*Ian Hesford signed for Sunderland from Sheffield Wednesday in August 1986. He was the first choice goalkeeper for two seasons prior to the arrival of Tony Norman.*

*Mick Buckley was a £60,000 signing from Everton in August 1978. His best season for Sunderland was 1981-1982 when he made 37 appearances.*

*Barry Venison's football league career started at Meadow Lane when he made his first team debut for Sunderland against Notts County on 10th October 1981. He played two hundred games for the club before moving to Liverpool for £200,000 in July 1986.*

*Reuben Agboola was signed by Len Ashurst from Southampton in 1985. A Nigerian international, Agboola stayed almost seven years at Sunderland.*

*Alan Kennedy in action during Sunderland's 2-0 win against Carlisle United at Roker Park on 8th February 1986. Left back Kennedy scored both goals that day.*

*Gary Bennett pictured during his early years as a Sunderland player. He was signed from Cardiff City by manager Len Ashurst in 1984 and by the time he left the club in 1995 had served under seven managers.*

*Some of the Third Division championship team celebrating a 4-1 away victory — and promotion — at Rotherham on 7th May 1988.*

*Paul Lemon in action against Rotherham United in a match which Sunderland won 4-1 and with the victory, the Third Division championship.*

*Paul Hardyman in action against West Ham United on 24th March 1990. He scored one of Sunderland's goals that day in a 4-3 home win. He arrived from Portsmouth on 11th July 1989 in a £130,000 deal and was later transferred to Brisol Rovers, three years to the day, for £160,000 having made 123 appearances for Sunderland.*

*Terry Butcher in action against West Ham United on 27th February 1993.*

*Peter Davenport moved from Middlesbrough to Sunderland in a £300,000 deal during the 1990-1991 close season. He was an ever present during the 1992 F.A. Cup run when Sunderland were beaten 2-0 by Liverpool in the final.*

# 1977-1978

The close season departure of team captain Tony Towers to Birmingham City and only one win in the first ten games sent Roker Park attendances plummeting. Supporters became disenchanted at the number of ex Burnley Football Club personnel arriving at Roker. As well as manager Jimmy Adamson and his assistant Dave Merrington, ex Burnley player Ken Knighton joined the club as first team coach and Mick Docherty had joined the club as a player on New Years Eve 1976 from Manchester City although he formerly played for Burnley.

Results generally improved as the season progressed but Sunderland did not play consistently well enough to be considered as serious promotion contenders. They finished the season in sixth position and twelve points behind third placed Tottenham Hotspur who were promoted with Bolton Wanderers and Southampton.

It was disappointment all round in both cup competitions with Sunderland bowing out of the League Cup and F.A. Cup at first attempts to Middlesbrough and Bristol Rovers respectively.

**Incoming players included:**
Gordon Chisholm, Wayne Entwhistle, Roland Gregoire, Wilf Rostron, Alan Weir

**Outgoing players included:**
Doug Collins, Alan Foggon, Billy Hughes, Dick Malone, Ian Porterfield, Trevor Swinburne, Tony Towers, Colin Waldron

**Sunderland's league record read:**

| P | W | D | L | F | A | Pts | Position |
|----|----|----|----|----|----|-----|----------|
| 42 | 14 | 16 | 12 | 67 | 59 | 44  | 6th      |

League appearances (with F.A. Cup and League Cup appearances in brackets): Armstrong 7, Arnott 21 (1), Ashurst 38 (3), Bolton 36 (3), Brown 6, Clarke 23 (1), Collins 2 (1), Docherty 26 (3), Elliott 25 (2), Entwhistle 7 (1), Gilbert 14, Greenwood 15, Gregoire 5, Henderson 32 (2), Hindmarch 2, Holden 11 (1) Kerr 36 (2), Lee 32 (2), Rostron 33 (3), Rowell 38 (3), Siddall 42 (3), Stronach 2, Waldron 8 (2), Weir 1

Average home attendances: 22,650

*English international Steve Whitworth who joined Sunderland from Leicester City in 1978.*

*Following yet another frustrating season of disappointment, Argus took stock of the situation in his concluding Roker Reflections page of the Sunderland Football Echo for the 1977-1978 season. "Manager Jimmy Adamson is entitled to feel that a lot of ground work has been done towards putting together a team which can be a credit to the club. And though they finished in sixth place and twelve points adrift of a promotion position last season, it was still quite a performance. There is a clear difference of opinion between those fans who demand instant success and those who accept that team building is a time taking job. The argument goes that for a club of Sunderland's standing the last two seasons – and how many before that – have mounted to abject failure, relieved only by the 1973 F.A. Cup triumph and a promotion success in 1976 1977 which was too fragile to last. A positive viewpoint says that Jimmy Adamson has a full new season to develop the ideas which seemed to be coming right at the end of the season. Next must come the financial backing to complete the building of a side not only with promotion potential but good enough to go higher still. Investment would put the finishing touches to the team and its splendid foundation and, at the same time, keep faith with the fans whose belief in the club has been stretched to breaking point."*

# 1978-1979

Despite looking the part of Second Division champions for most of the season, Sunderland had to be content with an end of season league placing of fourth and an agonising one point short of promotion.

A splendid run of seven wins from eight games in the second half of the season, starting with a 4-1 win at St. James' Park, had promotion looking a formality. However, two defeats from the final three home games were instrumental in condemning Sunderland to a further season in the Second Division.

Sunderland's away form left nothing to be desired. A run of fourteen away games undefeated created a new club record but it was a different story on home soil where they lost more home games than in all but one of their fourteen seasons of Second Division football.

Sunderland's poor form in the League Cup continued with a 2-0 first round home defeat by Stoke City while an exciting 2-1 victory against Everton in the F.A. Cup was followed by elimination by Burnley in the fourth round.

Jimmy Adamson resigned as manager on 25th October 1978 whereupon he joined Leeds United. Despite some encouraging performances under his management, Adamson suffered an uneasy relationship with a section of Sunderland supporters and this was undoubtedly one of the reasons behind his resignation. Adamson's assistant, Dave Merrington, was immediately appointed caretaker manager and his record of four wins and two draws from eight games was creditable. He resigned his position on 11th December and was replaced by Billy Elliott for the remainder of the season. It was always felt that Elliott's appointment was a stop-gap arrangement and that nothing less than promotion would have landed him the job on a permanent basis. Billy Elliott's record of four defeats in twenty three games should have been enough to land him the job but his contract was not renewed at the end of the season.

**Incoming players included:**
Mick Buckley, John Cooke, Rob Hindmarch, Ian Hughes, Ian Watson, Steve Whitworth.

**Outgoing players included:**
Roy Greenwood, Mel Holden, Bobby Kerr, Peter Stronach.

**Sunderland's league record read:**

| P | W | D | L | F | A | Pts | Position |
|---|---|---|---|---|---|-----|----------|
| 42 | 22 | 11 | 9 | 70 | 44 | 55 | 4th |

League appearances (with F.A. Cup and League Cup appearances in brackets): Arnott 15 (2), Ashurst 10 (1), Bolton 32 (4), Brown 14, Buckley 30 (1), Chisholm 27 (2), Clarke 33 (3), Coady 3, Docherty 26 (2), Elliott 41 (4), Entwhistle 34 (4), Gilbert 12 (1), Greenwood 3 (1), Gregoire 1, Henderson 30 (4), Kerr 3 (1), Lee 30 (3), Rostron 34 (3), Rowell 32 (4), Siddall 41 (3), Watson 1 (1), Whitworth 10.

Average home attendance: 25,545

*Shaun Elliott was a tower of strength in the Sunderland defence for ten seasons.*

*Roker Reflections at the end of the season saw Argus pondering the likely outcome of the managerial vacancy and he left no doubts in the minds of Sunderland Football Echo readers that he favoured a continuation of the Billy Elliott and Ken Knighton partnership. Argus wrote, "The vast majority of those supporters who backed the club during the second half of the season have left no doubt that they believe the Billy Elliott/Ken Knighton combination to be good for Sunderland. A change of manager can have a profound effect on how a team fares, regardless of how well it may be equipped in the matter of players. Values change with individuals and progress made under one manager can be swept aside by the advent of a different outlook. It can cut both ways of course and there is recent proof at Roker Park with Bob Stokoe leading Sunderland to a Wembley triumph with what was basically Alan Brown's team. Equally, Elliott and Knighton have profited by the team building of Adamson and Merrington although it should not be forgotten that two players who have been encouraged back to exciting form, Kevin Arnott and Alan Brown, had been virtually discarded by Adamson and Merrington. Sunderland directors will decide without being influenced by outside sources whether they want to change from a certain present to nebulous future. Theirs is the power and theirs the responsibility."*

# 1979-1980

Much of the close season activity centred around media speculation on the vacant manager's job. Following the club's announcement that Billy Elliott's contract was not being renewed, many big names were linked with the job. For whatever reason, the position had not been filled by late June and the job was offered to ex first team coach Ken Knighton who readily accepted.

Ken Knighton's first activity was to appoint Nottingham Forest's Frank Clark as assistant manager. He made two significant signings before the start of the season; Chris Turner form Sheffield Wednesday and Bryan Robson from West Ham United for his second spell with the club. Both proved to be astute signings. Chris Turner won the battle of the goalkeepers when challenging Barry Siddall keeper's shirt; Turner playing in thirty of the club's forty two league games. Meanwhile, Robson scored twenty league goals to become the club's leading goalscorer of the season.

On several occasions Sunderland embarked upon a goal scoring spree and emphatic victories over Charlton Athletic (4-0 on two occasions), Q.P.R. (3 0), Oldham Athletic (4-2), Burnley (5-0) and Watford (5-0) helped to sustain the promotion challenge and send them into the last game of the season needing only a draw to guarantee promotion. A crowed of 47,129 packed into Roker Park for the game against F.A. Cup winners West Ham United and cheered Sunderland on to a 2-0 victory — and promotion — with goals from Kevin Arnott and Stan Cummins.

Ken Knighton's team building towards the promotion goal had worked well and it was disappointing to see average attendances rise by less than one thousand. One exception to Knighton's successful signings was that of Argentine International player Claudio Marangoni whose signing in December 1979 was heralded as something of a coup at the time. Marangoni was unable to adapt his obvious skills to Sunderland's style of play and he left for South America in January 1981.

There was excitement in the League Cup with successful ties against Newcastle United and Manchester City. Both ties required replays and the Newcastle game was settled only after a penalty shoot out. Sunderland then met West Ham United in a 1-1 draw at Roker Park before the London team won the replay 2-1 at Upton Park.

There were few thrills in the F.A. Cup; Bolton Wanderers winning by the only goal of the game in the third round tie at Roker Park.

**Incoming players included:**
Stan Cummins, Barry Dunn, John Hawley, Joe Hinnigan, Claudio Marangoni, Bryan Robson, Chris Turner

**Outgoing players included:**
Jackie Ashurst, Mick Docherty, Wayne Entwhistle, Roland Gregoire, Mick Henderson, Wilf Rostron, Alan Weir

**Sunderland's league record read:-**

| P | W | D | L | F | A | Pts | Position |
|---|---|---|---|---|---|-----|----------|
| 42 | 21 | 12 | 9 | 69 | 42 | 54 | 2nd |

League appearances (with F.A. Cup and League Cup appearances in brackets): Arnott 37 (4), Ashurst 2 (1), Bolton 22 (4), Brown 29 (5), Buckley 17 (4), Chisholm 12 (3), Clarke 39 (7), Cooke 4, Cummins 26 (1), Dunn 15 (2), Elliott 41 (7), Entwhistle 2 (1), Gilbert 8 (4), Hawley 9 (2), Hindmarch 21 (2), Hinnigan 14, Hughes 1, Lee 7 (3), Marangoni 16 (1), Robson 40 (5), Rostron 8 (3), Rowell 8 (4) Siddall 12 (6), Turner 30 (1), Whitworth 42 (7)

*Kevin Arnott was a player of tremendous natural ability who many supporters felt did not realise his full potential. He made his Sunderland debut in the 1976-1977 season.*

Average home attendance: 27,399

*"Sunderland Are Back" was the back page headline of The Sunderland Echo on 13th May 1980, the day after Ken Knighton's team regained their First Division status.*

*The Sunderland Echo reported that the team were back in the First Division after three seasons in the soccer wilderness and as the champagne flowed Knighton said, "I will make sure that we stay there. The sky is the limit and we must build on what we have achieved. I brought in better players than we had to win promotion and if it means buying again to stay up then I will do so."*

# 1980-1981

The season started well with a 3-1 home win against Everton and a 4-0 success at Manchester City. Sunderland lost only three of their twelve opening games and the feeling within Roker Park was one of quiet optimism. However seven defeats in the next nine games saw Sunderland in their more traditional First Division position near the foot of the table.

Despite subsequent encouraging victories over Arsenal (2-0), Manchester United (2-0), Norwich City (3-0) and Coventry City (3-0), results were generally disappointing and Ken Knighton and Frank Clark were sacked following disagreements with club chairman Tom Cowie. The decision to sack the management duo was taken on 11th April 1981 with just four league games remaining and was one of the strangest in the entire history of Sunderland A.F.C.

Mick Docherty was placed in temporary control of team selection with just four games remaining. He experienced victory in two of those games including the crucial final game of the season at Anfield. Few, if any, of the club's supporters attributed Sunderland's survival to astute leadership or to the decision to rock the managerial boat so late in the season.

There was no cheer in either the League Cup or F.A. Cup competitions. Sunderland lost out to Stockport County and Birmingham City respectively, both defeats taking place in replays at Roker Park.

**Incoming players included:**
Sam Allardyce, Ian Bowyer, Tom Ritchie, Colin West.

**Outgoing players included:**
Mick Coady, Tim Gilbert, Bob Lee, Claudio Marangoni, Bryan Robson.

**Sunderland's league record read:**

| P | W | D | L | F | A | Pts | Position |
|---|---|---|---|---|---|-----|----------|
| 42 | 14 | 7 | 21 | 58 | 53 | 35 | 17th |

League appearances (with F.A. Cup and League Cup appearances in brackets): Allardyce 24 (2), Arnott 34 (4), Bolton 39 (4), Bowyer 9, Brown 28 (3), Buckley 15, Chisholm 33 (4), Cooke 14 (1), Cummins 42 (4), Dunn 1, Elliott 38 (4), Hawley 16 (4), Hindmarch 29 (3), Hinnigan 16 (1), Marangoni 3 (1), Ritchie 14, Robson 9, Rowell 26 (2), Siddall 15, Turner 27 (4), Vincent 1, Whitworth 29 (3).

Average home attendance: 26,139

*Claudio Marangoni became Sunderland's first big money import when Ken Knighton signed the Argentine international in 1979.*

*At the end of the 1980-1981 season, The Sunderland Football Echo urged the Sunderland directors to act swiftly and decisively in coming up with a permanent successor to Ken Knighton. Tribute was paid to Mick Docherty for the manner in which he accepted responsibility for maintaining First Division status and for the bold approach which he brought to the task.*

## 1981-1982

Alan Durban was appointed manager of Sunderland A.F.C. during the close season and set about his task by signing Iain Munro and Ally McCoist.

The change of manager failed to arrest the staple diet of mediocrity on the field with Sunderland winning just one of their first fourteen games and scoring a miserly seven goals, five of which were scored in the opening two games. Two goals in twelve games was hardly crowd pulling form and it spoke volumes for the patience of Sunderland's supporters that the average home attendance during this barren spell was 25,613.

In total, the season's goal scoring exploits totalled thirty eight which was the worst since the dark days of the 1969-1970 relegation season.

The season was one of constant relegation fear without even the consolation of a good cup run. Sunderland defeated Rotherham United in their first round ties of both the League Cup and F.A. Cup but failed to progress any further. Crystal Palace ended Sunderland's interest in the League Cup by winning 1-0 at Roker Park while Liverpool's visit ended in a 3-0 victory for the Merseysiders in the F.A. Cup.

**Incoming players included:**
Ally McCoist, John McGinley, Iain Munro, Nick Pickering, Mark Prudhoe, Barry Venison.

**Outgoing players included:**
Sam Allardyce, Kevin Arnott, Joe Bolton, Ian Bowyer, Barry Dunn, John Hawley, Ian Hughes, Ian Watson, Steve Whitworth.

**Sunderland's league record read:**

| P | W | D | L | F | A | Pts | Position |
|---|---|---|---|---|---|-----|----------|
| 42 | 11 | 11 | 20 | 28 | 58 | 44 | 19th |

This was the first season in which three points were awarded for a win.

League appearances (with F.A. Cup and League Cup appearances in brackets):
Arnott 6 (2), Bowyer 6 (1), Brown 5, Buckley 37 (4), Chisholm 20 (1), Clarke 25 (6), Cooke 8, Cummins 35 (6), Elliott 36 (6), Hindmarch 36 (4), Hinnigan 30 (1), McCoist 19 (4), McGinley 3, Munro 34 (3), Nicholl 3 (2), Pickering 37 (5), Ritchie 18 (5), Rowell 30 (6), Siddall 23 (6), Turner 19, Venison 17 (2), West 13 (1), Whitworth 2 (1).

Average home attendance: 19,072

*Alan Durban signed Ally McCoist from St. Johnstone for £400,000 in August 1981.*

*Following Sunderland's last game of the season, a 1-0 home win over Manchester City which finally erased fears of relegation, comment in The Sunderland Football Echo the following Saturday reasoned that the team's record during the final eleven games of the season — six wins, three draws and two defeats — gave every justification to believe that a mid table position was a realistic target for 1982-1983. Alan Durban's end of season comment was, "This side is good enough to finish in the middle of the table next season. Things can only get better with a younger side who have spent most of the season learning the game. We have got to keep our best players and add to the squad to win anything but we will never be in this position again."*

## 1982-1983

Sunderland marginally improved their league record by finishing the season in fifteenth position with fifty points. This was four league places and six points better than in the previous season. Relegation fears once again surfaced well before the end of the season although the team finally pulled three points clear of the dreaded drop.

Alan Durban's policy of signing experienced players to blend with youth was only moderately successful. The signings included Jimmy Nicholl who had joined the club on loan during the previous season.

Although finishing in their highest league position since 1967-1968, supporters were not impressed with the standard of entertainment and voted with their feet by staying away. The average home attendance was the lowest for eleven years.

In the League Cup, Sunderland survived the tie against Wolverhampton Wanderers but lost out to Norwich in the next round. In the F.A. Cup, Sunderland could only manage a goalless draw at home to Manchester City in the third round but lost the replay 2-1 at Maine Road.

**Incoming players included:**
Ian Atkins, Leighton James, Jimmy Nicholl, Frank Worthington.

**Outgoing players included:**
Alan Brown, Jeff Clarke, Joe Hinnigan, John McGinley, Jimmy Nicholl, Tom Richie, Barry Siddall.

**Sunderland's league record read:**

| P | W | D | L | F | A | Pts | Position |
|---|---|---|---|---|---|-----|----------|
| 42 | 12 | 14 | 16 | 48 | 61 | 50 | 15th |

League appearances (with F.A. Cup and League Cup appearances in brackets): Atkins 36 (5), Buckley 18 (4), Chisholm 32 (3), Cooke 11 (3), Cummins 29 (3), Elliott 20 (5), Hindmarch 14 (2), Hinnigan 3, James 18, McCoist 19 (4), Munro 37 (4), Nicholl 29 (6), Pickering 39 (5), Proctor 5, Prudhoe 7, Rowell 34 (6), Turner 35 (6), Venison 36 (5), West 19 (4), Whitfield 3, Worthington 18 (1).

Average home attendance: 17,013

*Nick Pickering played in a variety of positions for Sunderland during a five year period between 1981 and 1986.*

*Following the end of the 1982-1983 season, The Sunderland Football Echo summarised the season's signings and concluded that Alan Durban had few equals in the transfer market. The summary highlighted the deal which brought Ian Atkins to Sunderland as one of the steals of the season. Ian Atkins cost Sunderland £30,000 plus the signature of Alan Brown. The signing of Frank Worthington from Leeds United for £50,000 was also seen as a shrewd buy, given the part he played in Sunderland's successful fight against relegation. Finally, The Sunderland Football Echo concluded, the biggest influence over the latter part of the season was the acquisition of Leighton James on a free transfer from Swansea City.*

# 1983-1984

This was yet another season during which Sunderland saw a change of manager. The season started on what was by now a familiar low note with four defeats in six games. A temporary improvement saw just two defeats in the next ten games. However the away fixture at Notts County on 10th December 1983 brought Durban and his team down to earth — a 6-1 defeat against a side who spent most of the season in a relegation position and who were ultimately relegated nine points adrift of First Division safety. After just two victories in the next eleven league games, Alan Durban was sacked and became the tenth Sunderland manager to leave the club since the 1946-1947 season.

Durban's successor was quickly named as ex-Sunderland player Len Ashurst. He got off to a winning start with a 1-0 home win against Q.P.R. but four wins, three draws and five defeats in the remaining games meant that Sunderland were once again dependant upon winning their last game of the season in order to avoid relegation. The all important game at Leicester City was won 2-0 thanks to goals from Bryan Robson and Lee Chapman.

For the second successive season, Sunderland lost out to Norwich City in the League Cup, after having disposed of Cambridge United in the previous round. A 3-0 away success against Bolton Wanderers in the thrid round of the F.A. Cup, with goals from Rowell, West and Chapman, was followed by a 2-1 defeat against Birmingham City at Roker Park and the end of Sunderland's interest in the competition for another season.

**Incoming players included:**
Paul Atkinson, Paul Bracewell, Lee Chapman, David Corner, John Cornforth, Paul Lemon, John Moore, Mark Proctor, Bryan Robson.

**Outgoing players included:**
Mick Buckley, Ally McCoist, Iain Munro, Frank Worthington.

**Sunderland's league record read:**

| P | W | D | L | F | A | Pts | Position |
|---|---|---|---|---|---|-----|----------|
| 42 | 13 | 13 | 16 | 42 | 53 | 52 | 13th |

League appearances (with F.A. Cup and League Cup appearances in brackets): Atkins 40 (5), Atkinson 7, Bracewell 38 (6), Chapman 14 (2), Chisholm 36 (6), Cooke 1 (1), Elliott 33 (5), Hindmarch 12 (1), James 32 (5), Munro 9 (1), Murray 1, Pickering 42 (6), Proctor 40 (6), Robson 7, Rowell 31 (6), Turner 42 (6), Venison 41 (5), West 36 (5).

Average home attendance: 16,009

*Local lad Colin West scored 28 goals for Sunderland between 1981 and 1985.*

# Football Echo
### SUNDERLAND
SATURDAY, MAY 11, 1985. No. 35,259 (112th Year). 14p

# 9,398 BID FAREWELL

## 'We must bounce back'

SUNDERLAND manager Len Ashurst made it perfectly clear in today's club programme the need to bounce back to the First Division at the first attempt by saying: "The bottom line has finally emerged at the end of a topsy-turvy season and that is the unfortunate fact of being relegated.

"The pain is very hard to take for everybody with the club at heart and certainly at this juncture I am not going to delve into the reasons how we attained a Wembley appearance followed by six weeks of demise and deterioration which has put us into the Second Division.

"What has emerged from within the club is an inner strength from all concerned and an overwhelming obligation after what has happened to get the club back into the First Division at the first attempt. Anything else would be unsatisfactory. That is our aim.

"Once again, how we do it will only unfold during the course of the summer months. I am certainly not delving into the players' contracts issue at present. Our local press will keep you, our supporters, up to date with the facts that emerge during the negotiations which will take place during the course of the next week or two, and obviously with the addition of new players."

### THE TEAMS

| SUNDERLAND | IPSWICH |
| --- | --- |
| 1 Turner | 1 Cooper |
| 2 Cornforth | 2 Burley |
| 3 Pickering | 3 Gernon |
| 4 Bennett | 4 Zondervan |
| 5 Armstrong | 5 Cranson |
| 6 Berry | 6 Butcher |
| 7 Cooke | 7 Putney |
| 8 Wallace | 8 Brennan |
| 9 Hodgson | 9 D'Avray |
| 10 Lemon | 10 Wilson |
| 11 Atkinson | 11 Gates |
| Sub: Elliott | Sub: Yallop |

Referee: Mr D. Richardson (Great Harwood)

## SUNDERLAND .................... 1
## IPSWICH TOWN ................. 2

A PATCHED-UP Sunderland side fought hard to make a winning finale to the First Division against an Ipswich side striving for their own survival but it was not to be.

Before the lowest league crowd at Roker Park in 11 seasons they were beaten by a last minute goal from Kevin Wilson who had earlier put Ipswich in the lead.

Ian Wallace had equalized in the 21st minute — the first league goal scored by Sunderland at Roker Park in 606 minutes — but they never really looked like getting another and for the brilliance of Chris Turner would have been beaten out of sight.

### Geoff Storey reports from Roker Park

Sunderland, again ravaged by injuries, introduced 17-year-old John Cornforth for his First Division debut and recalled John Cooke and Paul Atkinson. Barry Venison (hamstring), Gordon Chisholm (hamstring) and Clive Walker (groin), joined Reuben Agboola, Peter Daniel, Stan Cummins and Howard Gayle on the injured list while skipper Shaun Elliott took over as substitute despite not being fully recovered from an Achilles tendon injury.

In the absence of Elliott and Venison the player of the year Chris Turner captained Sunderland for the first time and having won the toss set an unchanged Ipswich side the task of attacking the Fulwell end. Armstrong lined up alongside Bennett in central defence with Cornforth at right back.

Sunderland's problems increased immediately from the kick off when Butcher clattered into Hodgson, himself a doubtful starter, and the Sunderland striker needed attention before play resumed with a free kick.

### Goal lines

| | |
| --- | --- |
| Wilson | 17 min. |
| WALLACE | 21 min. |
| Wilson | 89 min. |

Wallace showed neat control before finding Cooke who was hopelessly off target with a long range drive. Ipswich came back with a clever ball from Gates almost letting in D'Avray who was foiled by an important interception by Cornforth.

Gates was guilty of a glaring miss in the 16th minute when completely miskicking in front of goal but a minute later Ipswich were ahead when WILSON, receiving from Gates, cut inside to beat Turner with a low drive.

After Sunderland had won the first corner in 20 minutes Ipswich came close to increasing their lead. Wilson beat Pickering but Atkinson was able to knock the ball behind for a corner.

It was from the clearance that Sunderland went on to level terms in the 21st minute. Hodgson did well to shake off Butcher and find the unmarked WALLACE who closed in to lob the ball over the advancing Cooper to score Sunderland's first league goal at Roker Park in 606 minutes.

Zondervan easily shook off Cooke and when his drive cannoned off Bennett, Wilson was quickly to the rebound. Though he went down when challenged by Cornforth the referee was not impressed with Ipswich's claims for a penalty.

Ipswich were near to regaining the lead in the 29th minute when Burley crossed from the right and though Gates struck the ball well enough from close range Turner went down quickly to his right to make a brilliant save.

Putney wasted a great opportunity. The winger beat Pickering, cut inside, only to blaze the ball across the face of goal when he had time and space to close in.

### TV SOCCER

TV SOCCER
B.B.C. TONIGHT
MATCH OF THE DAY
Southampton v Coventry
Man. City v Charlton
ITV TOMORROW
THE BIG MATCH
Q.P.R. v Man. United
Norwich v NEWCASTLE

Millwall promoted

Manchester City promoted from Second Division. Cardiff and Notts County join Wolves as the relegated clubs.

## Fire sweeps stand

THIRTY people were injured today when fire swept through the main stand at Bradford City's football ground. Spectators among the 10,000 crowd fled as a strong breeze fanned flames towards the offices and dressing rooms.

Play was held up without any score and the match was abandoned.

More than 100 firemen fought the blaze.

About 30 casualties were taken to three hospitals, some with serious burns.

Police insisted the fire was not a deliberate arson attempt and had been started by a fan playing with matches at the back of the main grandstand, which held around 3,000 supporters.

● Second half of Birmingham's Second Division game against Leeds started 33 minutes late after fighting between rival supporters at half-time. See back page.

OPEN SPACE: The gaps on the terraces tell their own story of a sad end to a First Division season at Roker Park.

Turner had to race from his line to prevent Wilson reaching a through ball from Gernon.

Ipswich kept up the pressure with a right wing cross from Burley being met in front of goal by Wilson who failed to connect cleanly and Turner was relieved to find the ball travelling outside the upright.

### HALF-TIME

| | |
| --- | --- |
| SUNDERLAND | 1 |
| IPSWICH | 1 |

Sunderland were soon on the move after the restart with a right wing cross from Cooke being chested down by Hodgson who initially was in space but was finally crowded out by the visitors' defence.

Hodgson failed to make contact with a spectacular flying header to an Atkinson centre and then was outjumped by Cranson after Turner had easily dealt with a chip shot from Gates. Cooper was almost deceived by a deep cross-cum-shot from Atkinson, turning the ball over for a corner.

It almost led to Sunderland going ahead in 61 minutes when the ball eventually came back to Atkinson the winger's shot dipped just too late though there were many in the crowd who thought that the ball had gone in.

The referee had a quiet word with Zondervan and Bennett following a midfield flare up which resulted in a free-kick to Sunderland.

In the 74th minute Ipswich brought on Yallop for Gernon but before Sunderland could bring on Elliott, Armstrong was penalized a couple of yards outside the penalty area for a push on D'Avray. Though Gates bent the free-kick past the wall Turner was down quickly to make another good save.

Elliott came on for Bennett in 77 minutes, the substitution not affecting the balance of the side, just one injured player replacing another.

Two minutes later it was Turner to the rescue again. The goalkeeper made a brilliant stop from Yallop and from the rebound threw himself at the feet of Wilson to prevent a certain goal.

Turner came to the rescue again punching behind when a high centre from Yallop was headed down by D'Avray for the ever-alert Wilson to be denied again. The heroics from Turner continued with Gates rolling the ball into the path of Yallop whose powerful low drive was beaten out by Turner and the save brought tremendous applause from all parts of the ground.

There was just no way past Turner who somehow denied Brennan in 86 minutes with another tremendous close range save when all seemed lost.

The winner which Ipswich so richly deserved came in the last minute when WILSON took a return pass from Butcher to close in and hammer the ball wide of Turner and just inside the upright.

### FINAL

| | |
| --- | --- |
| SUNDERLAND | 1 |
| IPSWICH | 2 |

Attendance: 9,398

Pools check

*Sunderland's fourth spell in Division One ended in 1985. The McMenemy era was about to dawn and the Third Division would soon be beckoning.*

# 1984-1985

As had been predicted in the Sunderland Football Echo, the season was one of comings and goings with Len Ashurst dismantling the nucleus of Alan Durban's side to finance a re-building programme.

It was the season when Sunderland supporters had their first real taste of bargain basement transfers. Incoming players such as Berry, Gayle, Walker, Cummins, Wallace and Wylde were all brought to the club for small fees and most left within a year or so for lesser fees or on free transfers. In order to finance the alleged spending spree, players of the calibre of Ian Atkins, Paul Bracewell, Gary Rowell, Lee Chapman and Bryan Robson were allowed to leave the club. This `sell one good player and buy three mediocre ones' policy truly established Sunderland as a second class club.

Three defeats in the first thirteen league games was encouraging form although the more cynical supporters were not convinced that good times were just around the corner as home attendances failed to reach even nineteen thousand. The inconsistent side of the team's nature became apparent as they then proceeded to win just four of their next twenty two league games. Sunderland's abysmal performance againt Leicester City at Roker Park in early December resulted in a 4-0 defeat and set the alarm bells ringing that another struggle against relegation was a distinct probability.

The fight against the drop proved to be one too many and the club were deservedly relegated with a meagre forty points, nine less than Norwich City who finished the season immediately above them.

Instant dismissal from the F.A. Cup following a 4-0 defeat at Southampton was more than compensated for by the team's League Cup results. Sunderland's defeats of Crystal Palace, Nottingham Forest, Tottenham Hotspur, Watford and Chelsea made a nonsense of the team's league form and set up a Wembley showdown with Norwich City in the final of the competition. The game was a non event for Sunderland, an own goal by Gordon Chisholm and a missed penalty by Clive Walker settling the game in Norwich City's favour.

Following assurances from the club chairman that his job was safe, Len Ashurst was sacked as manager on 24th May 1985 when he became one of the few managers to be relieved of his duties only weeks after leading out his team at Wembley.

As club chairman Tom Cowie began his search for a new manager, Sunderland A.F.C. was about to enter the darkest period of its history.

**Incoming players included:**
Reuben Agboola, Gordon Armstrong, Gary Bennett, Steve Berry, Stan Cummins, Peter Daniel, Cameron Duncan, Howard Gayle, David Hodgson, Clive Walker, Ian Wallace, Dale White, Roger Wylde.

**Outgoing players included:**
Ian Atkins, Paul Bracewell, Lee Champman, Rob Hindmarch, Leighton James, Mark Prudhoe, Bryan Robson, Gary Rowell, Colin West, Roger Wylde.

**Sunderland's league record read:**

| P | W | D | L | F | A | Pts | Position |
|---|---|---|---|---|---|-----|----------|
| 42 | 10 | 10 | 22 | 40 | 62 | 40 | 21st |

League appearances (with F.A. Cup and League Cup appearances in brackets): Agboola 8, Armstrong 3, Atkinson 5 (1), Bennett 37 (9), Berry 31 (11), Chisholm 31 (10), Cooke 4 (1), Corner 3 (2), Cummins 13, Daniel 25 (10), Elliott 31 (7), Gayle 19 (7), Hodgson 23 (7), Lemon 10, Moore 3, Pickering 37 (8), Proctor 17 (5), Turner 42 (11), Venison 39 (11), Walker 38 (10), Wallace 14 (1), West 20 (5), Wylde 8 (4).

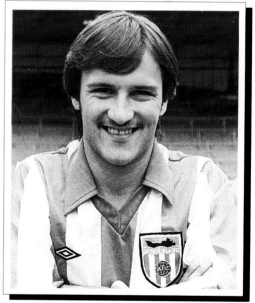
*Stan Cummins signed for Sunderland on two occasions.*

Average home attendance: 18,464

*At the end of a most disappointing season, The Sunderland Football Echo made the valid point that while success in the League Cup had gone a long way towards wiping out the club's overdraft, at the end of the day the cash generated had turned out to be fool's gold as it was not used to strengthen the team. Given the fact that most players want success, it would have been much easier to have persuaded them to join Sunderland with the twin towers of Wembley as the bait than with the certainty of Second Division football. The feature continued to say that although the club would make every effort to keep the squad together to form the basis of the promotion push there were four players who were at liberty to leave Sunderland under the Freedom of Contract. The players concerned — Shaun Elliott, Gordon Chisholm, Mark Proctor and Chris Turner — had all been offered new terms but could well wish to keep their options open in an attempt to continue their careers within the First Division. The Sunderland Football Echo said that it made a sad sight to see discarded season tickets falling from the stands at the end of the season with many supporters vowing never to return.*

Towards the end of the season, former Sunderland skipper Ian Atkins was rapped in public by Everton manager Howard Kendall for unflattering remarks about his old club in a Sunday newspaper feature. In the feature he accused Sunderland of "Penny pinching and thinking like a Fourth Division club when they should be in the top six every week." While Atkins' outburst was condemned by Kendall, the newspaper concerned did not receive a deluge of letters from Sunderland supporters criticising Atkins or rushing to the club's defence.

Sunderland, ravaged by injuries recalled John Cooke and Paul Atkinson to the side while handing a first team debut to John Cornforth. Ipswich made most of the early running and were unlucky not to score when a neat pass from Gates to D'Avray was intercepted by Cornforth. Gates was in the thick of the action and should have scored in the 16th minute but he was back in the next minute with a great ball to Wilson who cut inside to beat Turner with a low drive. After Atkinson conceded a corner, the ball was cleared upfield and Hodgson shook off Butcher to find the unmarked Wallace who lobbed the ball over Cooper to score Sunderland's first league goal at Roker Park in six hundred and six minutes. Ipswich dictated play for the remainder of the half and should have scored when Putney blazed the ball over from close range.

Sunderland almost took the lead in the 61st minute when an Atkinson shot dipped just too late to go into the net with the goalkeeper beaten. Turner came to the rescue in the 77th minute when he saved brilliantly from Yallop and from the rebound he threw himself at the feet of Wilson. It was all one way traffic by now and Turner again denied Ipswich a goal with an unbelievable close range save from Brennan. Ipswich were finally rewarded for their attacking play when Wilson took a return pass from Butcher to finally beat Turner from close range. The lowest Roker Park crowd for eleven seasons, 9,398, bid farewell to the First Division as Sunderland were relegated.

**Sunderland:** Turner, Cornforth, Pickering, Bennett, Armstrong, Berry, Cooke, Wallace, Hodgson, Lemon, Atkinson.

**Ipswich:** Cooper, Burley, Gernon (Yallop), Zondervan, Cranson, Butcher, Putney, Brennan, D'Avray, Wilson, Gates.

# 1985-1986

The appointment of Lawrie McMenemy as manager of Sunderland Football Cub was met with unprecedented adulation. Supporters thronged the streets surrounding Roker Park to welcome Big Mac as their saviour.

McMenemy immediately attempted to repeat the successful formula from his Southampton days and signed a string of experienced former international players. In came George Burley, Eric Gates, Frank Gray and Alan Kennedy. Out went Nick Pickering, Gordon Chisholm and Chris Turner.

Events on the field were disastrous. Sunderland made their worst ever start to a season. Five straight defeats, ten goals conceded and none scored saw Sunderland dumped at the bottom of the Second Division. Despite the mass hysteria surrounding McMenemy's appointment, only 21,208 attended the opening game of the season; a home fixture with Blackburn Rovers. By the time the third home game came around on 7th September 1985, the attendance of 14,985 may have suggested that McMenemy's charisma was already becoming tarnished.

With a series of on-loan goalkeepers in the side — McDonagh, Bolder (who eventually signed) and Dibble — and a run of results which included eight single goal victories in the first twenty five games, the club was rapidly becoming a laughing stock in the eyes of many North East football fans.

Sunderland's first tie in the League Cup under McMenemy was against Swindon Town and ended in defeat. In the F.A. Cup, a home win against Newport County was followed by defeat against Manchester United.

Results failed to improve and a sequence of just one league victory between 18th Janaury and 12th April meant that relegation to the Third Divison was a distinct possibility. Three of the club's last four fixtures were at Roker Park and victory in all three games guaranteed Second Division survival which triggered unbelievable after match scenes which embarrassingly culminated in a lap of honour from the team and an on-pitch appearance by McMenemy.

**Incoming players included:**
Bob Bolder, George Burley, Eric Gates, Frank Gray, Steve Hetzke, Alan Kennedy, Nigel Saddington, David Swindlehurst.

**Outgoing players included:**
Steve Berry, Gordon Chisholm, John Cooke, Stan Cummins, Peter Daniel, Nick Pickering, Chris Turner, Clive Walker, Dale White.

**Sunderland's league record read:**

| P | W | D | L | F | A | Pts | Position |
|---|---|---|---|---|---|-----|----------|
| 42 | 13 | 11 | 18 | 47 | 61 | 50 | 18th |

League appearances (with F.A. Cup and League Cup appearances in brackets): Agboola 12 (4), Armstrong 13, Atkinson 10 (3), Bennett 28 (2), Berry 1, Bolder 22 (5), Burley 27 (4), Chisholm 1, Corner 9 (3), Daniel 8 (1), Dibble 12, Duncan 1, Elliott 32 (1), Ford 8, Gates 38 (3), Gayle 20, Gray 32 (3), Hetzke 8, Hodgson 10 (1), Kennedy 32 (5), Lemon 4, McDonagh 7, Moore (1), Pickering 22 (3), Proctor 19 (3), Swindlehurst 25 (3), Venison 36 (5), Walker 10 (2), Wallace 14 (3), White 2.

Average home attendance: 16,634

*Eric Gates arrived from Ipswich before the start of the 1985-1986 season and stayed at Roker for five years.*

# 1986-1987

Club chairman Tow Cowie resigned before a ball was kicked and Bob Murray took over the hot seat.

The season saw public opinion turning against McMenemy following a string of indifferent performances, poor results and a belief that the manager's financial package did not represent value for money.

There was no doubting the fact that team performances left much to be desired and results spoke for themsleves. The season opened brightly with a 2-0 win at Huddefield Town. This was followed by a disappointing 1-1 home draw with Brighton and a 6-1 drubbing at Blackburn Rovers who had finished the previous season one place beneath Sunderland in the Second Division.

A 2-0 home win over Birmingham City on 25th October sent Sunderland soaring to fifth position in the Second Division — the pinnacle of McMenemy's achievements at Roker Park. Thereafter it was downhill all the way with one win in the next ten games. As Sunderland plunged deeper and deeper into the relegation mire, a run of five defeats, one draw and an attendance of 8,544 for the home defeat by Sheffield United on 11th April resulted in the removal of McMenemy from the manager's hot seat. During his time as Sunderland A.F.C.'s manager, McMenemy's league record was:

| P | W | D | L | F | A | Pts |
|---|---|---|---|---|---|-----|
| 77 | 23 | 21 | 33 | 86 | 109 | 88 |

Bob Stokoe was immediately installed as caretaker boss with the thankless task of attempting to preserve the club's Second Division status and while team performance improved, it was asking too much of Stokoe to cure the ills of the previous two seasons in the space of five games. A penalty miss by Mark Proctor in the home game with Barnsley contributed to Sunderland's defeat and subsequent condemnation to the promotion/relegation play-offs. A two legged tie against Third Divison Gillingham produced a shock 3-2 away defeat for Sunderland and although they managed a 4-3 home victory over the Kent side, Stokoe's men lost out on the away goal rule. The unthinkable had happened. For the first time in their proud history Sunderland had been booted into the Third Division wilderness.

In the League Cup, McMenemy's Sunderland were eliminated from the competition at the first attempt by minnows York City while there was instant dismissal from the F.A. Cup by Wimbledon.

**Incoming players included:**
Keith Bertschin, David Buchanan, Terry Curran, Steve Doyle, Iain Hesford.

**Outgoing players included:**
Bob Bolder, Shaun Elliott, Howard Gayle, David Hodgson, Barry Venison, Ian Wallace.

**Sunderland's league record read:**

| P | W | D | L | F | A | Pts | Position |
|---|---|---|---|---|---|-----|----------|
| 42 | 12 | 12 | 18 | 49 | 59 | 48 | 20th |

League appearances including play-off games (with F.A. Cup and League Cup appearances in brackets): Agboola 11 (2), Armstrong 42 (2), Atkinson 3 (1), Bennett 43 (3), Bertschin 13, Buchanan 24 (2), Burley 27 (2), Corner 17 (1), Curran 9, Doyle 35 (1), Duncan (2), Gates 24 (3), Gray 40 (3), Hesford 40 (1), Hetzke 23, Kennedy 24 (1), Lemon 32 (2), Mimms 4, Moore 1, Outterside 1, Proctor 32 (3), Saddington 3 (1), Swindlehurst 36 (3).

Average home attendance; 13,924

*In its obituary on 18th May 1987, The Sunderland Echo described Sunderland's relegation as "a disgrace" and referred to the prospect of Third Division football as being "unthinkable and unforgiveable". The report continued to say that the writing had been on the wall for months and that disaster had been inevitable with too much damage to the team having been done during a second successive season under Lawrie McMenemy. Devastated Sunderland fans sobbed bitterly on the terraces as their team dropped into the lower reaches of football. Then as shock turned to anger many directed their frustration at both players and directors.*

*Frank Gray was signed by Lawrie McMenemy from Leeds United in July 1985 and survived the manager at Sunderland by two years.*

Sunday 17th May 1987 was the blackest day in the illustrious history of Sunderland A.F.C. It was the day that the club was relegated to the Third Division for the first time in its 108 year existence.

During the final game of the season, the play-off against Gillingham, Sunderland's fans were magnificent in their vocal support, cheering their side even when things started to go badly wrong. The players responded superbly as they bombarded the Gillingham goal. They had left it too late, however. Too many half hearted performances earlier in the season had finally caught up with them.

As the big drop became reality, distraught fans cried openly on the terraces and in the streets surrounding Roker Park. Bob Murray promised "We will be back". A heartbroken Bob Stokoe, who almost pulled off the impossible during his nine match run as caretaker manager, discounted himself from the job of full time manager saying that he was ten years too old to accept the challenge of restoring Sunderland to their rightful place in soccer's elite.

# SUNDERLAND 4 GILLINGHAM 3 (after extra time)
### Aggregate score 6-6 (Gillingham won on away goals rule)

The blackest day yet in the club's history saw Gillingham condemn the once proud Rokermen to a season in third class league football. With Gillingham attacking from the start, it was no surprise when the Kent side took an early lead through a Howard Pritchard header. It took a goal from Eric Gates, when he picked up a pass from Alan Kennedy, to put the passion into Sunderland's play and five minutes later Gates put Sunderland in front when he headed home a Gordon Armstrong cross. When a Gillingham player handled David Swindlehurst's header on the line it looked as if the game was going Sunderland's way but Mark Proctor's spot kick hit Phil Kite's legs.

When Ian Hesford upended Pritchard, the pendulum seemed to be swinging in Gillingham's favour and although the Sunderland goalkeeper beat out the resulting penalty he could do nothing about Tony Cascarino's shot following Trevor Quow's cross from the rebound. As the minutes ticked by it looked as if Sunderland were a beaten side when Gary Bennett headed an 88th minute equaliser on aggregate and forced the game into extra time.

Three minutes into extra time an unmarked Cascarino restored Gillingham's aggregate lead and although a flying header from Keith Bertschin raised Roker hopes, it was not sufficient to prevent Sunderland losing out on the away goals rule.

**Sunderland:** Hesford, Lemon, Kennedy (Corner), Doyle, Gray, Bennett, Armstrong, Proctor, Bertschin, Swindlehurst, Gates.

**Gillingham:** Kite, Haylock, Pearce, Berry, Quow, Greenall, Pritchard, Weatherley (Shearer), Smith, Elsey, Cascarino.

# 1987-1988

Denis Smith breezed into Roker Park to confidently predict promotion into the Second Division at the first attempt and such was his confidence that he offered to contribute towards the compensation due to his former club York City, to whom he had been under contract, if Sunderland failed to win promotion.

Sunderland chairman Bob Murray's reaction to the disaster suffered at the hands of the previous so called big name manager had been to appoint the relatively unknown management duo of Denis Smith and Viv Busby as his successor. It turned out to be a master stroke as Smith's Sunderland took the division by storm and won the championship with the greatest of style.

Mr. Smith's knowledge of the lower division was emphasised by several bargain basement incoming transfers including Marco Gabbiadini, Colin Pascoe, John MacPhail and John Kay.

The striking partnership of Gabbiadini and Gates was the most exciting that the Third Division had ever seen with crowds, unprecedented at that level of football, flocking to the games to see the champions elect. Average attendances at home rocketed by almost three and a half thousand compared with the previous season in the Second Division.

The Gabbiadini/Gates strikeforce produced forty goals, only one team had a meaner defence and a record-breaking ninety three points were accumulated en route to the Second Division.

The season was not without it disappointments with Sunderland bowing out of the Leauge Cup to Middlesbrough and suffering a shock F.A. Cup defeat at Scunthorpe United. However, Sunderland were single minded in their pursuit of escape from the Third Division wilderness and dreams of cup successes were happily cast aside for one season.

**Incoming players included:**
Tim Carter, Marco Gabbiadini, Mickey Heathcote, John Kay, John MacPhail, Richard Ord, Gary Owers, Colin Pascoe.

**Outgoing players included:**
David Buchanan, Terry Curran, Steve Hetzke, Alan Kennedy, Mark Proctor, Nigel Saddington, David Swindlehurst.

**Sunderland's league record read:**

| P | W | D | L | F | A | Pts | Position |
|---|---|---|---|---|---|-----|----------|
| 46 | 27 | 12 | 7 | 92 | 48 | 93 | 1st |

*John MacPhail was a bargain £23,000 signing by Denis Smith in July 1987.*

Legue appearances (with F.A. Cup and League Cup appearances in brackets): Agboola 37 (4), Armstrong 36 (3), Atkinson 21 (2), Bennett 38 (3), Bertschin 14 (2), Buchanan 1, Burley (1), Carter 1, Corner 4, Cornforth 8, Doyle 31 (2), Gabbiadini 35 (2), Gates 42 (4), Gray 12, Hardwick 6 (2), Hesford 39 (2), Kay 46 (3), Lemon 35 (3), MacPhail 41 (4), McGuire 1, Ord 4 (1), Owers 37 (4), Pascoe 8, Proctor 4 (2).

Average home attendance: 17,340

# SPORTS Echo

SATURDAY, APRIL 30, 1988. No. 36,166 (115th Year). 18p

# CHAMPIONS!

## Gates winner clinches the title for Roker

**PORT VALE** .................................. **0**   **SUNDERLAND** ................................. **1**

**SUNDERLAND turned in a championship-winning performance to roar back into the Second Division at the first attempt.**

They outclassed Port Vale in every department, though it took until the 79th minute before they made the vital breakthrough with Eric Gates's 20th goal of the season.

Leading goalscorer Marco Gabbiadini in particular was out of luck as goalkeeper Mark Grew produced a series of brilliant saves, while Iain Hesford at the other end was virtually a spectator so much were Sunderland in command.

A point at home to Northampton on Monday night will make absolutely certain of the title — but even if Sunderland were to lose both their remaining matches, Walsall would have to win their last two games by an aggregate 19-0 to deny them the Third Division trophy.

Both sides were unchanged, Sunderland relying on the team that thrashed Mansfield 4-0 in midweek and Port Vale on the 11 that dented Wigan's promotion hopes with a 2-1 win.

Port Vale won a first minute corner when Beckford cut in from the right only to be checked by MacPhail. Hesford easily cut out the flag kick, but the home side were soon back with Beckford and Riley linking up in play. It looked dangerous until Riley, under pressure from Bennett, shot wide.

Gray had Sunderland on the move with a long through ball which had Armstrong in pursuit, but Webb managed to get the ball into touch. Armstrong's long throw drifted behind before Bennett could make contact.

Gabbiadini needed treatment in the sixth minute when he was caught in the back by a rash challenge from Sproson, who was promptly booked. From MacPhail's free kick, Gabbiadini won in the air without being able to direct his header on target.

### Brilliant save

Sunderland almost grabbed the lead in eight minutes. Lemon started the move, bringing in Gabbiadini, who cleverly beat Sproson and crossed to the far post. Armstrong failed to connect cleanly, but he set up Gates whose first-time effort from close range was brilliantly turned behind by Grew.

It was all Sunderland, with another corner quickly following and when this was only partially cleared, Gray released Bennett wide on the left. It took a diving header by Webb to prevent the ball reaching the unmarked Gates and Gabbiadini.

Twice within the space of a minute centres from Pascoe were met by Gabbiadini. The leading goalscorer headed into the side-netting from a difficult angle when he should have knocked the ball back. Then a brave diving header cleared the bar.

A Lemon centre was misjudged by Webb, catching Bennett by surprise. The ball bounced off Ben-

**by Geoff Storey at Vale Park**

nett's legs and went harmlessly behind. But at this stage Sunderland had grabbed the initiative. Gabbiadini set off on a surging run, but Gates shot wide when the ball broke loose.

In a rare home attack Walker linked up with Ford. From the right wing centre Riley failed to get any power behind his close range effort, leaving Hesford to make a comfortable catch.

Sunderland were soon back, however, with Lemon finding Gates, who almost got Armstrong in the clear. Sproson took the sting out of the move by getting the ball back to Grew.

Grew came to Port Vale's rescue again in the 25th minute with another brilliant save. A mistake by Hazell let in Pascoe. He rolled the ball into the path of Lemon, whose first-time effort from only about 12 yards was beaten out by the goalkeeper.

Beckford got free on the right, but although he had Earle and Riley up in support, his attempt to find either of his colleagues in front of goal was foiled by Bennett.

Sunderland were continually being caught offside, Gabbiadini in particular failing to master the home defence's tactics. Lemon just managed to stay onside and then keep the ball in play, but his centre failed to trouble Grew.

In 37 minutes a bad mistake by Bennett let in Beckford and the Sunderland defence was wide open when a shooting chance was set up for Ford, whose first-time effort was a shade too high.

Port Vale were gradually getting back into the game and following a flowing move, Ford had a close-range snap-shot comfortably saved by Hesford.

In 42 minutes Lemon released Gabbiadini on the right, but after shaking off Hazell, Gabbiadini twice failed to get the ball in the middle after reaching the by-line.

**Half time: Port Vale 0, Sunderland 0**

**COLIN PASCOE — a leading role in Sunderland's final drive to glory at Port Vale**

Sunderland made a bright start on the resumption, winning a free kick just outside the penalty area when Hazell held off Gabbiadini. Lemon's inswinger to the far post was headed out by the diving Hughes.

The home side replied through Beckford, whose shot on the run was comfortably dealt with by Hesford. Kay was hopelessly off target with a 25-yard effort and after Doyle had battled to win the ball in midfield, Gates failed to bring in Pascoe.

Hazell handled a first-time flick-on from Pascoe and was promptly booked in 54 minutes. From the free kick MacPhail's header almost deceived Grew, who made a last-gasp save at the foot of the post at the expense of a corner.

Bennett was a shade too cool in allowing a hopeful through ball to travel on to Hesford. Riley was quickly in to gain possession, but he lifted his shot over the bar.

Gabbiadini had a shot deflected behind for a corner following neat touches by Pascoe and Lemon. Armstrong's inswinger was turned behind by Walker and when he tried again the ball was headed out.

Armstrong then linked up with Lemon, and from his centre Gabbiadini brought another brilliant save out of the diving Grew.

Doyle came to the rescue when Riley attempted to capitalise on a mistake by Kay, but the pressure was soon back on at the other end, with Grew having to race out of his area to clear from Gabbiadini.

**Continued in page 2**

### Goal lines

GATES.................. 79 min

| PORT VALE | SUNDERLAND |
|---|---|
| 1 Grew | 1 Hesford |
| 2 Webb | 2 Kay |
| 3 Hughes | 3 Gray |
| 4 Walker | 4 Bennett |
| 5 Hazell | 5 MacPhail |
| 6 Sproson | 6 Doyle |
| 7 Ford | 7 Lemon |
| 8 Earle | 8 Pascoe |
| 9 Riley | 9 Gates |
| 10 Beckford | 10 Gabbiadini |
| 11 Mills | 11 Armstrong |
| Subs: Maguire | Subs: Agboola |
| Steggles | Cornforth |
| Ref: K Cooper (Pontypridd) | |

*Denis Smith rescued Sunderland from the Third Division wilderness at the first attempt as the team were promoted in 1988.*

# 1988-1989

The first six matches back in the Second Division revealed that any thoughts of promotion for the second successive season were somewhat optimistic. The first six league games failed to produce a victory. Denis Smith kept faith with his Third Division championship side with the only significant additions to the squad being Whitehurst, Norman and Hauser; the latter two not arriving until the second half of the season.

By mid season it was clear that Second Divison consolidation was a more realistic target than promotion. Sunderland's mid table stature was confirmed in every sense; sixteen wins, fifteen draws and fifteen defeats with sixty goals both scored and conceded gave Sunderland an eleventh placing in a league of twenty four teams.

Supporters were entitled to expect more from the domestic cup competitions. After disposing of York City by an aggregate 4-0 scoreline in the League Cup, Sunderland were drawn against fellow Second Division promotion hopefuls West Ham United. A disastrous 3-0 defeat in the first leg at Roker Park left Sunderland with too big a mountain to climb in the return match at Upton Park. They lost that game by a more respectable 2-1 scoreline but were out of the League Cup for another season. In the F.A. Cup, Sunderland were held to a 1-1 draw at home to Oxford United but lost the replay 2-0.

**Incoming players included:**
Brian Atkinson, Peter Barnes, Tony Cullen, Riccardo Gabbiadini, Thomas Hauser, Warren Hawke, Alan Hay, Tommy Lynch, Tony Norman, Sean Wharton, Billy Whitehurst, Paul Williams.

**Outgoing players included:**
Keith Bertschin, George Burley, John Cooke, Ian Hesford, John Moore, Billy Whitehurst.

**Sunderland's league record read:**

| P | W | D | L | F | A | Pts | Position |
|---|---|---|---|---|---|-----|----------|
| 46 | 16 | 15 | 15 | 60 | 60 | 63 | 11th |

Richard Ord played his first game for Sunderland on 3rd November 1987.

League appearances (with F.A Cup and League Cup appearances in brackets):
Agboola 25 (3), Armstrong 45 (6), Atkinson 2, Barnes 1, Bennett 37 (5), Carter 2, Cornforth 10, Cullen 3, Doyle 35 (6), Gabbiadini 35 (6), Gates 27 (6), Gray 36 (4), Hauser 6, Hawke 1, Hay 1, Hesford 20 (4), Kay 11 (3), Lemon 12 (2), Lynch 4, MacPhail 45 (6), Norman 24 (2), Ord 31 (3), Owers 36 (4), Pascoe 39 (6), Wharton 1, Whitehurst 17.

Average home attendance: 14,707

*In the end of season Sunderland Sports Echo, Sunderland manager Denis Smith reflected upon the club's first season back in the Second Division and in some ways he considered it a season of might have beens. Principally it was a case of what might have been if Marco Gabbiadini had not been sent off twice during the season and missed seven games as a result. With Gabbiadini out of the side, Sunderland struggled to find the net. In all, he missed eleven league games in which Sunderland scored nine goals (an average of 0.8 goals per game). In the remaining thirty five games, with Gabbiadini in the team of fifty one goals were scored (an average of almost 1.5 goals per game). Clearly, Marco Gabbiadini gave pace to the forward line and was a real handful to defenders. It was his absence and Sunderland's inability to replace him when he was suspended or injured that cost Sunderland a top six position and a place in the play offs.*

# 1989-1990

A campaign which culminated in promotion via a most unorthodox route. From the first day of the season when Sunderland won convincingly 2-0 at Swindon Town, the red and whites looked promotion material.

The close season signing of Paul Hardyman had tightened up the defence while Paul Bracewell's return to the club from Everton introduced some much needed culture into midfield. Only one defeat in the first ten games and just four by the mid-point of the season had supporters dreaming of promotion. Despite a loss of form in early 1990, Sunderland rarely slipped out of the promotion pack and it came as a major disappointment to finish the season in sixth position.

With sixth position came a two legged play-off tie against third placed Newcastle United. A goalless draw at Roker Park was followed by a Sunderland victory at St. James' Park with goals from Gabbiadini and Gates in one of the most exciting derby matches ever played. The prize was a place at Wembley against Swindon Town who had defeated Blackburn Rovers in the other play off tie.

The Wembley final was a game in which Sunderland were outplayed and totally outclassed by Ossie Ardiles' Swindon team. The result, 1-0 to Swindon Town, flattered Sunderland and condemned them to another season of Second Division football, or so it was thought. An investigation by the Football League and the Inland Revenue into allegations of illegal payments being made by the Wiltshire club to its players had the outcome of Swindon being relegated and their place in the First Division passing to the beaten play-off finalists, Sunderland.

Sunderland enjoyed their best season in the League Cup since their Wembley appearance in 1984-1985. A 4-1 aggregate win against Fulham was followed by victories over Bournemouth and Exeter (in both cases after replays) and a quarter final draw against Coventry City. Following an evenly balanced game at Roker Park which ended goalless, Sunderland travelled to Highfield Road for the replay in confident mood. With two enforced changes from the first game (Sunderland were without MacPhail and Pascoe), Sunderland were completely outplayed and beaten 5-0. In the F.A. Cup, the club played just one game; a 2-1 defeat at Reading.

**Incoming players included:**
Paul Bracewell, Kieron Brady, Martin Gray, Paul Hardyman

**Outgoing players included:**
Peter Barnes, Steve Doyle, Frank Gray, Alan Hay, Tommy Lynch

**Sunderland's league record read:**

| P | W | D | L | F | A | Pts | Position |
|---|---|---|---|---|---|-----|----------|
| 46 | 20 | 14 | 12 | 70 | 64 | 74 | 6th |

League appearances including play-off games (with F.A. Cup and League Cup appearances in brackets): Agboola 33 (5), Armstrong 49 (9), Atkinson 11 (3), Bennett 39 (8), Brady 9, Bracewell 39 (5), Carter 18 (8), Cornforth 1 (1) Cullen 5, Gabbiadini M 49 (8), Gates 37 (9), Hardyman 43 (7), Hauser 6 (1), Hawke 2, Heathcote 6, Kay 34 (6), Lemon 1 (1), Lynch 1 (1) MacPhail 41 (5), Norman 31 (1), Ord 6 (3), Owers 46 (9), Pascoe 33 (8), Williams 1 (1)

Average home attendance: 17,408

*A bargain buy by Denis Smith from York City, Marco Gabbiadini cost Sunderland £80,000 in 1987.*

*At the end of the league season, The Sunderland Sports Echo highlighted mediocre home form as the main reason behind Sunderland's failure to secure an automatic promotion spot. While there were only two teams in the Second Division with better away records, no fewer than nine clubs won more home points than Sunderland managed at Roker Park. The newspaper made the point that ten victories in twenty three home games was simply not good enough for a side chasing promotion to the top flight and that the side must adapt to coping with opponents who are obsessed with defensive minded tactics on away soil. Just as importantly, the feature concluded, the players must come to terms with playing in front of a demanding crowd, yearning for success after years in the soccer wilderness.*

**Division 2 (Second Leg) Play-Offs 1989-1990 | NEWCASTLE UNITED 0   SUNDERLAND 2**

For the fourth time in the season, Newcastle United finished second best to Sunderland. With the Newcastle strike force of Quinn and McGhee being well shackled by Bennett and MacPhail it was always going to be an uphill struggle for the black and whites once Eric Gates had opened the scoring. A John Kay throw-in was flicked on by Gabbiadini to Owers who raced for the goal-line. From his cross, Gates hit the ball into the net for his first goal of the year. Owers almost increased Sunderland's lead in the 27th minute when he exchanged passes with Gabbiadini but United's Burridge was alert to the situation.

Sunderland dominated midfield in the second half just as they had done in the first and when Bracewell found Gabbiadini with a great ball, the Sunderland striker was unlucky not to score. With Newcastle's only threatening moves coming from set pieces, Sunderland looked in confident mood throughout and could have put the game beyond doubt when Owers was just beaten to the rebound off a Burridge save from Gabbiadini. Sunderland wrapped up the game after 85 minutes when Warren Hawke laid the ball off for Gabbiadini to pass to Gates who closed in to force a low shot beyond Burridge.

**Newcastle United:** Burridge, Scott, Stimson, Aitken, Anderson, Bradshaw (Dillon), Brock, Askew (O'Brien), Quinn, McGhee, Kristensen.

**Sunderland:** Norman, Kay, Agboola, Bennett, MacPhail, Owers, Bracewell, Armstrong, Gates, Gabbiadini, Hawke.

# Sports Echo

SATURDAY, MAY 11, 1991. No. 37,091 (118th Year).  24p

# DOWN

**MANCHESTER CITY** ............................. **3**
**SUNDERLAND** ................................... **2**

## Quinn double seals sad fate

SUNDERLAND were relegated back to the Second Division in a pulsating finish to the season.

While Luton were beating Derby, the Rokermen crashed to defeat at Manchester City.

But Sunderland had their chances and will be disappointed they did not beat a City side who were given the cost of a tenth-minute lead through Niall Quinn.

Sunderland grabbed a 40th-minute equaliser through Marco Gabbiadini. Four minutes later Gary Bennett put them ahead.

But Quinn equalised in the next minute and although Sunderland dominated the second half Gabbiadini was guilty of at least two glaring misses.

David White sealed their fate by scoring City's winner in the last minute, but with Luton beating Derby it didn't really matter.

**MATCH REPORT AND PICTURES, CENTRE PAGES**

MARCO GABBIADINI scored Sunderland's first goal and might have had a first-half hat-trick at Maine Road. But in the second half he was guilty of some awful misses.

### Darlo champs, Pool promoted

DARLINGTON are the Fourth Division champions.

Hartlepool have also won promotion to Division Three for the first time since 1968-69.

Pool beat Northampton Town 3-1 at home thanks to Paul Dalton, Joe Allon and Paul Baker. Rivals Blackpool slipped up, 2-0 at Walsall.

Darlington overcame Rochdale at Feethams. David Cork fired a ninth minute opener, with Frank Gray adding a 46th minute penalty.

● Pool report on page 2

### Harford helps out his old club

SUNDERLAND-born Mick Harford helped send his home-town club down.

His own goal five minutes before half-time put his old team Luton in the driving seat at home to Derby. And that set them on the way to pulling off their third successive last-day escape.

Luton attacked right from the first whistle, making chance after chance. Danish striker Lars Elstrup confirmed their victory when he put them 2-0 up with a close-range header two minutes after the break.

**MIDDLESBROUGH and NEWCASTLE reports on centre pages**

*Sunderland's return to the First Division in 1990 lasted just one year. Failure to invest in team strengthening had this predictable result.*

# 1990-1991

Boardroom promises to strengthen the side with quality signings did not materialise and it was the failure of Sunderland's directors to capitalise on the good fortune of promotion via the back door which rankled with supporters for many seasons.

The only transfer activity prior to the start of the season involved the arrivals of Kevin Ball from Portsmouth and Peter Davenport from Middlesbrough. Indeed, these were the only two significant signings for the entire season and so a team which was good enough to finish no higher than sixth position in a mediocre Second Division was asked to cope with the demands of First Division football. It was hardly surprising that they failed.

In a slimmed down First Division of twenty clubs, Sunderland won just eight of their thirty eight league games. Relegation stared them in the face from the beginning of the season with just two wins from the first thirteen games. There could be no doubting the effort or commitment of the players or of the management duo of Smith and Busby. The basic fact that the first team squad was not good enough was apparently acknowledged by everyone except the Sunderland Board of Directors who contented themselves with laying plans for a new all seater stadium near the A19.

Sunderland's brief flirtation with First Division football ended after just one season in the top flight when they were relegated along with Derby County. It was a thoroughly miserable season in both the League Cup and F.A. Cup too, following a 6-0 defeat at Derby County and a 2-1 reversal at Arsenal, respectively.

**Incoming players included:**
Kevin Ball, Peter Davenport, Brian Mooney, David Rush, Anthony Smith

**Outgoing players included:**
Riccardo Gabbiadini, Eric Gates, Mickey Heathcote, Paul Lemon, John MacPhail

**Sunderland's league record read:**

| P | W | D | L | F | A | Pts | Position |
|---|---|---|---|---|---|-----|----------|
| 38 | 8 | 10 | 20 | 38 | 60 | 34 | 19th |

League appearances (with F.A. Cup and League Cup appearances in brackets): Agboola 5, Armstrong 35 (4), Atkinson 4, Ball 33 (4), Bennett 37 (4), Bracewell 37 (4), Brady 4 (1), Carter 1, Cornforth 1, Cullen 2, Davenport 27 (3), Gabbiadini 30 (3), Hardyman 30 (3), Hauser 5 (1), Hawke 3 (1), Kay 28 (4), MacPhail 1, Mooney 5, Norman 37 (4), Ord 12, Owers 38 (4), Pascoe 25 (1), Rush 8 (1), Smith 9 (2), Williams 1

Average home attendance: 21,925

*Colin Pascoe was a bargain £70,000 buy from Swansea City in 1988.*

*"Six relegations in thirty three years is a sad reflection on Sunderland's former glory years," stated The Sunderland Football Echo on 18th May 1991. The statement followed confirmation of Sunderland's relegation at Maine Road after Manchester City's 3-2 victory despite an all-out effort by the Sunderland team which included goals from Gabbiadini and Bennett.*

# 1991-1992

For a while it looked as if the unthinkable might happen for a second time and Sunderland would be relegated to the Third Division. Seven defeats in eight games during the final third of the season set the alarm bells ringing but the potential crisis was averted with Sunderland finishing the season in eighteenth position.

After a mixed bag of results in the first nine games — three wins, two draws and four defeats — Sunderland took the decision to cash in on their prize asset, Marco Gabbiadini. The player had been accused by the club of losing his way but had still managed to score five goals in nine games! A fee of £1,800,000 was agreed with Crystal Palace for the club's only natural goalscorer.

With cash in the transfer kitty, Denis Smith signed Anton Rogan from Celtic for £350,000 and John Byrne from Brighton for £225,000. Peter Beagrie was taken on loan from Everton and although his five appearances won rave reviews, Sunderland made little attempt to secure his signature. By December, Sunderland were back on the transfer trail and this time the subject of their interest was West Bromwich Albion striker Don Goodman who, after lengthy negotiations signed in a £900,000 deal.

With Byrne and Goodman up front, Sunderland suddenly looked a force to be reckoned with when, inexplicably, Denis Smith was sacked. With Viv Busby already out of the picture following an earlier disagreement with Smith, the club turned to coach Malcolm Crosby to take charge of the team. Crosby got off to a flying start with five straight wins, three in the league and two in the F.A. Cup, which won him the Divisional Manager Of The Month award. Although it was Crosby's achievement in guiding the club to Second Division safety which was responsible for landing him the job on a permanent basis, it was his masterminding of an epic F.A. Cup run which made the headlines.

Earlier in the season, Sunderland had been unceremoniously dumped out of the League Cup by Third Division Huddersfield Town. The 6-1 aggregate score had been one of the most humilating cup experiences in the club's history. In the F.A. Cup, it was a completely different story. After disposing of Port Vale at home (3-0) and Oxford United away (3-2), Sunderland met West Ham United at Roker Park. A 1-1 draw was followed by a 3-2 victory in the replay and a quarter final tie with Chelsea at Stamford Bridge where a John Byrne goal was enough to give Sunderland a creditable draw against the First Division side. The replay produced a pulsating game with Sunderland running out worthy 2-1 winners. The semi final draw paired Sunderland with Norwich City at Hillsborough, Sheffield and once again the match winner was John Byrne who scored the only goal of the game and in doing so wrote himself into the record books as having scored in every round up to and including the semi final. However there was to be no fairytale repeat of the 1973 F.A. Cup final this time. Sunderland's opponents Liverpool ran out worthy 2-0 winners.

On the credit side, Sunderland's financial position had been greatly improved as a reuslt of the F.A. Cup run and, with this income surely being made available to Malcolm Crosby for team strengthening, there was every chance that the club would mount a serious promotion challenge in 1992-1993.

**Incoming players included:**
John Byrne, Don Goodman, Anton Rogan, Craig Russell, Ian Sampson

**Outgoing players included:**
Reuben Agboola, John Conforth, Marco Gabbiadini

**Sunderland's league record read:**

| P | W | D | L | F | A | Pts | Position |
|---|---|---|---|---|---|-----|----------|
| 46 | 14 | 11 | 21 | 61 | 65 | 53 | 18th |

*Malcolm Crosby leads his team out at Wembley in the 1992 F.A. Cup Final.*

League appearances (with F.A. Cup and League Cup appearances in brackets): Agboola 1, Armstrong 40 (9), Atkinson 29 (8), Ball 31 (8), Beagrie 5, Bennett 38 (6), Bracewell 39 (10), Brady 4, Byrne 27 (8), Carter 2, Cullen 1, Davenport 25 (10), Gabbiadini 9, Goodman 20, Hardyman 29 (9), Hauser 5 (1), Hawke 2, Kay 41 (9), Mooney 6, Norman 44 (10), Ord 5, Owers 24 (4), Pascoe 12 (1), Rogan 33 (9), Rush 20 (7), Russell 1, Sampson 7 (1) Smith 2, Williams 4

Average home attendance: 18,437

*In congratulating Malcolm Crosby in landing the job as manager, the Sunderland Sports Echo rightly said that he had been rewarded for his hard work but continued to say that Crosby probably felt that he was still on trial and that the pressure would be on from day one. Most supporters were of the opinion that Malcolm Crosby's achievements in guiding the club to Wembley and to Second Division safety had shamed the club into giving him the manager's job on a permanent basis. He certainly deserved better than the scant, half hearted financial backing which he received from the club during his time in office.*

**League Cup (6th Round Replay) 1991-1992** **SUNDERLAND 2    CHELSEA 1**

Chelsea showed six changes from the team fielded at Stamford Bridge nine days earlier. The Londoners failed to take advantage of a strong wind at their backs in the early stages and paid the penalty after 20 mintes when Rush won possession and released Byrne who beat Elliott and cut inside the box before hitting a low drive. Beasant beat out the shot, only for the ball to rebound to Davenport who made no mistake. After a shot from Davenport on the turn just cleared the bar, Sunderland began to come under increasing Chelsea pressure. Tony Norman had to race out to head away from Kerry Dixon and in another confrontation between the two players, Norman punched away a header. Norman again came to the rescue when he denied Cascarino and then just on half time Dixon had a glorious opportunity to level the scores but failed to get a touch to Wise's centre in front of goal.

It was end-to-end football in the second half. Firstly, Norman made a great save from Dixon and after Beasant blocked a Davenport effort, Sunderland surged forward once again. This time, a fantastic run into the penalty area by Atkinson had the Chelsea defence in tatters and when Beasant pushed his shot aside, Davenport raced in to push the ball towards an empty net but Elliott somehow got back to clear.

Five minutes from time, Vinny Jones found Dennis Wise with a perfectly weighted pass and the £1.6 million signing grabbed his eleventh goal of the season. To their credit, Sunderland fought back in determined style and had the last say in the 88th minute when Atkinson's corner was met by Armstrong to make it 2-1 in Sunderland's favour.

**Sunderland:** Norman, Kay, Rogan, Ball, Hardyman, Rush, Bracewell, Davenport, Armstrong, Byrne, Atkinson.

**Chelsea:** Beasant, Clarke, Sinclair, Jones, Elliott, Cundy, Le Saux, Townsend, Dixon, Cascarino, Wise.

# 1992-1993

Yet another campaign when the club's supporters were left in limbo with a mid season change of management.

Manager Malcolm Crosby was given only a year in which to prove himself and, despite substantial income generated by the previous season's FA Cup run, he was given less than £1 million during the close season to re-shape a team which had just escaped relegation by the skin of its teeth. The close season decision, allegedly taken in Crosby's absence, to refuse Paul Bracewell the security of a two year contract and to subsequently allow him to join Newcastle United on Freedom of Contract was arguably the most costly mistake that the club made in modern times.

Free scoring John Byrne became unsettled at the club and was allowed to leave. With just four wins from the first sixteen games, Crosby came under increasing pressure. The team were leaking goals at an alarming rate: twenty seven in that opening sequence including a 6-0 defeat at West Ham United and a 5-2 reversal at Peterborough United. Crosby's last throw of the dice was to sign Terry Butcher on a free transfer, little knowing that within a matter of weeks Butcher would be succeeding him in the manager's hot seat. Malcolm Crosby was sacked after twenty five games and eight wins in the 1992-1993 season and the timing of the sacking — immediately after the Pools Panel defeat at Tranmere Rovers following the postponement of Sunderland's game there — gave ammunition to some sections of the popular press to question the credibility of the club's management.

Results under Terry Butcher were worse than under his predecessor with five wins from twenty one starts. Crosby's record for the season was 1.2 points per game compared with Butcher's haul of 0.95 points per game.

Sunderland found themselves in the familiar position of needing to win the final game of the season to survive. They were thrashed 3-1 by fellow relegation strugglers Notts County who, according to the Sunderland Sports Echo, "tore a sorry Sunderland to shreds." The final humiliation for Sunderland and their long suffering fans was the awareness that avoidance of the dreaded drop back to the Third Division had only been achieved courtesy of the failings of other teams on the final day of the season.

For the second successive season, Huddersfield Town ended Sunderland's interest in the League Cup at the first stage. In the F.A. Cup, victory over Notts County in the third round was followed by defeat in the next round at Sheffield Wednesday.

**Incoming players included:**
Terry Butcher, John Colquhoun, Shaun Cunnington, Michael Gray, Mick Harford, Lee Howey.

**Outgoing players included:**
Paul Bracewell, Kieron Brady, John Byrne, Tony Cullen, Paul Hardyman.

**Sunderland's League record read:**

| P | W | D | L | F | A | Pts | Position |
|---|---|---|---|---|---|-----|----------|
| 46 | 13 | 11 | 22 | 50 | 64 | 50 | 21st |

League appearances (with F.A. Cup and League Cup appearances in brackets)
Armstrong 41 (2), Atkinson 31 (2), Ball 43 (4), Bennett 14, Butcher 37 (4), Byrne 6 (2), Carter 13 (1), Colquhoun 12 (2), Cunnington 38 (4), Davenport 20 (1), Goodman 41 (3), Gray (Martin) 9. Gray (Michael) 23 (1), Harford 10, Kay 36 (4), Mooney 10 (2), Norman 33 (3), Ord 21 (3), Owers 33 (2), Rogan 12, Rush 12 (2), Sampson 4, Smith 7 (2).

Average home attendance: 16,988

*John Byrne spent only twelve months at the club during which time he played an important role in Sunderland's 1991-1992 F.A. Cup run.*

*The Sunderland Sports Echo predicted that the inquest into a disastrous campaign would linger well into the close season. The report continued to say that there could be few, if any, other football clubs which caused so much heartache to their supporters. The critics were having a field day in bombarding Bob Murray with their opinions — made all the more ferocious by the fact that they had spent all season living on the wake of Newcastle United's relentless pursuit of the First Division title.*

# 1993-1994

Despite his indifferent baptism to the Sunderland manager's job in the latter half of 1992-1993 season, Terry Butcher was given the green light to embark upon a spending spree on a scale unprecedented in Sunderland's history. Four close season signings were completed at a combined outlay of over £2 million.

Sunderland's start to the season was their worst in modern times; a 5-0 thrashing at Derby County although the team showed the other side of their character in the next game when they hammered Charlton Athletic 4-0 at Roker Park. A run of just one victory from the next six games and a subsequent five straight defeats resulted in Terry Butcher being shown the door. Once again, the club took the easy — and presumably cheap — option of appointing the new manager from the existing staff.

With Bob Murray standing down from the chairmanship, Mick Buxton was promoted from first team coach to manager and immediately brought in Trevor Hartley as his assistant. Sunderland lost their first game under Buxton but proceeded to win ten and lose only three of their next seventeen games which not only removed the perenial threat of relegation but prematurely raised hopes of achieving a play-off place. However, a dip in form removed all hope of aspiring to such dizzy heights and supporters had to content themselves with the safety of a mid table position.

The League Cup produced a 3-1 two legged victory over Chester City and two encouraging performances against Premiership team Leeds United, Sunderland winning by a 2-1 scoreline at both Roker Park and Elland Road. However any hopes of progressing to the latter stages of the competition were dashed in the next tie when Aston Villa emerged as emphatic 4-1 victors. In the F.A. Cup it took Sunderland a replay and extra time to dispose of Third Division Carlisle United only to see their interest in the competition end in the next round with a 2-1 away defeat at Wimbledon.

**Incoming players included:**
Alec Chamberlain, Derek Ferguson, Phil Gray, Andy Melville, Ian Rodgerson.

**Outgoing players included:**
Terry Butcher, Tim Carter, John Colquhoun, Peter Davenport, Mick Harford, Thomas Hauser, Warren Hawke, James Lawrence, Brian Mooney, Colin Pascoe, Anton Rogan, Paul Williams.

**Sunderland's league record read:**

| P | W | D | L | F | A | Pts | Position |
|---|---|---|---|---|---|-----|----------|
| 46 | 19 | 8 | 19 | 54 | 57 | 65 | 12th |

League appearances (with F.A. Cup appearances and League Cup appearances in brackets) Armstrong 22 (6), Atkinson 21 (4), Ball 36 (5), Bennett 37 (7), Chamberlain 43 (8), Cunnington 11 (1), Ferguson 41 (5), Goodman 34 (7), Gray (Martin) 16 (4), Gray (Michael) 16 (2), Gray (Phil) 39 (6), Howey 7 (1), Kay 3 (2), Kubicki 15, Lawrence 2, Melville 44 (8), Norman 3, Ord 24 (6), Owers 30 (8), Power 1 (2), Rodgerson 2, Russell 29 (1), Sampson 2, Smith (A) 1 (1), Smith (M) 27 (4).

*Roker stalwart Gordon Armstrong.*

Average home attendance: 17,212

*The end of season announcement in the Sunderland Sports Echo that the club's financial burden was being eased by a four year extension of the sponsorship deal with Vaux came with the all too familiar warning that there would be no lump sum payments for Mick Buxton to even contemplate transfer activity. Chairman John Featherstone commented that he remained optimistic of a cash injection into the club but said that there were no signs of a fairy godfather akin to Blackburn's Jack Walker on the horizon.*

## F.A. Cup (Third Round) 1993-1994 — SUNDERLAND 1  CARLISLE UNITED 1

With record signing Don Goodman and midfield maestro Martin Smith both returning to the side after injury, Sunderland were confident of overcoming Carlisle United who were forced to field third choice goalkeeper Tony Caig and were without star defender Paul Valentine. Two early chances fell to Phil Gray and Gordon Armstrong but when play switched to the other end the visitors were unfortunate not to take a surprise lead through Reeves. Carlisle were enjoying the best of the play in the first 25 minutes and the Sunderland defence were at full stretch to keep them out. In the 31st minute Sunderland took the lead against the run of play when an Armstrong cross was met by Gray before the ball broke loose to Ferguson who scored one of the easiest goals of his career.

In the second half Carlisle continued to press forward and looked the more dangerous side. Sunderland looked a disjointed team and were hanging on desperately to their slender lead. Smith and Armstrong switched wings in an effort to increase Sunderland's grip on the game but it came as no surprise when Carlisle's efforts were deservedly rewarded with an equaliser in the 80th minute. When Gray lost out to Edmondson, the ball broke quickly to Thomas whose low cross brought a fine save from Chamberlain although the Sunderland 'keeper could not hold on to the ball. Edmondson was on hand to hammer home the rebound. Incredibly, Carlisle were not content to settle for the draw and surged forward in search of the winner, although in the closing stages it was Sunderland who could have stolen it with half chances falling to both Goodman and Ord.

**Sunderland:** Chamberlain, Owers, Ord, Bennett, Melville, Smith, Ferguson, Ball, Armstrong, Goodman, Gray.

**Carlisle:** Caig, Burgess, Gallimore, Walling, Joyce, Edmondson, Thomas, Conway, Reeves, Davey, McCreery.

# 1994-1995

A promising start to the season saw Sunderland undefeated in the opening eight games; the first time that this had happened in post war years.

However, the team was far from being a settled one and goalscoring became a significant problem. Following the promise of the opening eight games Sunderland managed only seven wins from the next twenty nine games. Equally worrying was the fact that the team won only five home games all season and it came as no surprise when Mick Buxton became the ninth Sunderland manager in less than twenty years to be relieved of his duties. The latter statistic does not include managers who served the club in a caretaker capacity.

With Sunderland's interest in the League Cup being terminated at the first hurdle by Millwall and Tottenham Hotspur giving Sunderland a football lesson in the fourth round of the F.A. Cup when they won 4-1 at Roker Park (Sunderland had knocked out Carlisle United after a replay in the third round), the future looked bleak when Peter Reid was given seven games to save Sunderland from Second Division obscurity.

In short, Reid proved to be a breath of fresh air as his no nonsense approach earned him the immediate respect of both players and supporters. One defeat in seven games, against promoted Bolton Wanderers, not only saved Sunderland from relegation but it gave everyone connected with the club real hope for the future.

**Incoming players included:**
Steve Agnew, Brett Angell, Daruisz Kubicki, Martin Scott.

**Outgoing players included:**
Don Goodman, Gary Owers, David Rush, Ian Sampson

*Don Goodman in action against Millwall on 20th August 1994 when he scored Sunderland's goal in a 1-1 draw.*

**Sunderland's league record read:**

| P | W | D | L | F | A | Pts | Position |
|---|---|---|---|---|---|-----|----------|
| 46 | 12 | 18 | 16 | 41 | 45 | 54 | 20th |

League appearances (with F.A. Cup appearances and League Cup appearances in brackets): Angell 8, Agnew 16, Armstrong 10 (3), Atkinson 16 (1), Ball 42 (4), Bennett 19 (4), Broadie 1, Chamberlain 17 (3), Cunnington 3, Ferguson 23 (4), Goodman 17 (2), Gray (Martin) 17 (1), Gray (Michael) 10, Gray (Phil) 41 (5), Howey 6 (1), Kubicki 46 (5), Matteo 1, Melville 36 (4), Norman 29 (2), Ord 33 (2), Owers 18 (2), Rodgerson 3, Russell 28 (5), Scott 24 (3), Smith 33 (4), Snodin 6, Williams 3.

Average home attendance: 15,396

*Sunderland's slump from a best unbeaten start for eighty four years to their third worst finish sums up another sad chapter in the club's history according to the end of season post mortem in the Sunderland Sports Echo. The feature continued to say that to finish the season fifth from bottom of a moderate First Division won by near neighbours Middlesbrough was a bitter pill to swallow for Sunderland's magnificent supporters. Peter Reid had suggested at the successful conclusion to the seven game salvage operation that better times could be around the corner at Roker Park but the Sunderland Sports Echo suggested that unless Reid was given the financial tools to complete the job, competition would be as tough as ever in the escape out of the Second Division. The board of directors had made it clear that they were not about to embark upon a spend spend spend mission even though they admitted that the team needed strengthening. Although the shackles had been released without being completely freed two years ago when Terry Butcher was given more cash in one fell swoop than any other manager in the club's history, it seemed unlikely that Reid would be given even half that amount to spend as he set about his wheeling and dealing operation.*

**Division 1 1994-1995** | **SUNDERLAND 1    SHEFFIELD UNITED 0**

Peter Reid's first game in charge and a rousing wholehearted team performance in a howling wind and on a bone hard pitch. Sunderland tormented Sheffield United's defence in the first half as they surged forward with the wind behind them. They forced a series of corners but without a single clear cut chance falling to either side, a goalless first half was always on the cards.

An astute second half substitution saw a pacey Craig Russell replace a sluggish Brett Angell and the youngster's pace constantly had the Blades' defence at sixes and sevens. He was such a thorn in the side of centre back David Tuttle that the Sheffield United man was eventually dismissed for a professional foul. Sheffield United should have taken the lead in the 68th minute when Andy Scott was put clear but with only Tony Norman to beat he screwed his shot across the face of goal. Before the game, Peter Reid appealed to Roker supporters to be patient saying that he would settle for an 89th minute winner and that is exactly what Craig Russell provided as he forced the ball into the net with the game about to enter injury time.

**Sunderland:** Norman, Kubicki, Scott, Bennett, Ord, Atkinson, Agnew, Ferguson, Smith, Angell, Gray.

**Sheffield United:** Kelly, Gage, Nilsen, Hartfield, Tuttle, Beesley, Rogers, Veart, Whitehouse, Blake, Black.

# SPORTS ECHO

28p

*inside*

**GIVEN:** Brilliant keeper exceeds every hope

· page 4

**STEWART:** Fitness regime for Premier challenge

· page 5

**PROMOTION JOY:** Derby slip-up guarantees Premiership place

# GOING UP!

LOVELY BUBBLY!: Sunderland boss Peter Reid celebrates a glorious season, and promotion to the Premiership

**SUNDERLAND are up. Peter Reid's side clinched promotion to the Premiership this afternoon when Birmingham held Derby County to a draw at the Baseball Ground.**

The result meant that although Crystal Palace beat Wolves 2-0 at Molineux, Derby County could no longer catch the Rokermen and Wearside's party celebrations could get into full swing.

Reid was at Feethams to watch his former Manchester City sidekick Sam Ellis and ex-Sunderland coach Stan Ternant battle for crucial Third Division promotion points against Darlington.

But his thoughts were focused on the crucial games at Molineux and the Baseball Ground which have settled Sunderland's destiny to the delight of the manager.

"Without doubt this is as good as any moment I have enjoyed in football," said a cock-a-hoop Reid.

"A year ago we finished with 54 points and we were nearly relegated. I don't think anybody in their right minds would look a year on and see Sunderland Football Club in this position.

"I thought we would go near to the play-offs. We have to be realistic because we have done it without Martin Smith, David Kelly and Phil Gray for a fair bit of the season.

"I am delighted the way the season has gone and all I say to everybody connected with the club is enjoy it and don't even think about the Premiership.

"I will sort that out in the summer, just enjoy what we have done. This is a big club and the supporters, who have been brilliant, deserve the success we can now enjoy."

The waiting is over but Reid and his players will not be completely satisfied with their efforts over the last ten months until the First Division Championship has been won.

There will be no let-up in the target of maximum points from tomorrow's all-ticket home game with Stoke City.

Sunderland chase a club record of 17 unbeaten games at the expense of a Stoke side who have rarely been out of a play-off place all season.

"We've been in a limbo situation for the last few days just waiting for confirmation that we have done it," added Reid.

"But it's not all about what has happened today. It comes down to the fact we have lost six games out of 43 this season.

"That's the reason why we are top, not because of what anybody else has done. We are on a run since Lee Howey's late equaliser at Portsmouth and I can't stress just how important that goal was.

"I want to thank everybody, especially the players who have been magnificent. I am the front man but Paul Bracewell and Bobby Saxton have done tremendously well behind the scenes."

**Sunderland:** Chamberlain, Kubicki, Scott, Bracewell, Ball, Melville, Mick Gray, Ord, Russell, Howey, Agnew. Subs: Holl, Bridges, Aiston.
**Stoke City:** (from): Prudhoe, Clarkson, Sigurdsson, Whittle, Sandford, Devlin, Wallace, Gleghorn, Potter, Sheron, Sturridge, Beeston, Carruthers, Dreyer, Keen, Sinclair.

**DREAM TEAMS** *– how the title race is shaping up –* **PAGE 10**

*This Sports Echo headline tells its own story.*

# PROMOTION to the PREMIERSHIP

## 1995-1996

Peter Reid's first full season in charge and the one in which Sunderland almost forgot how to lose a game. When Reid miraculously saved the club from the ignominy of a second spell of third rate football in May 1995 even the most optimistic of Sunderland fans set their sights no higher than First Division respectability the following season.

However, with limited financial resources available to him, Peter Reid instilled his own special brand of self belief into each and every one of his players and in doing so he transformed them from a team of relegation candidates into one of championship winners. The numbers of consecutive wins, games without defeat and clean sheets tell their own story. No Sunderland team in living memory has played with such conviction.

Reid's first masterstroke was to persuade his former Everton midfield partner Paul Bracewell to rejoin the club. A modest transfer fee secured the Newcastle player's signature, not only as a player but also as Reid's number two. The quality and experience of the Roker backroom staff — Paul Bracewell, Bobby Saxton, Alan Durban, Bryan Robson and Ricky Sbragia — played a major part in Sunderland's success, a fact which Reid was quick to acknowledge   .

Ironically, the limited amount of cash that was made available to Peter Reid was spent on three players who had little opportunity to make major contributions to the season's success. Record-equalling signing David Kelly arrived from Wolverhampton Wanderers in a £900,000 deal but played only nine league games before an injury sustained on international duty finished his season. Injury restricted John Mullin to just five league appearances while the form of the Roker defence meant that Reid's only other major signing, Gareth Hall, managed only eight first team appearances.

The season saw Craig Russell and Michael Gray establish themselves as regular first teamers and the emergence of Michael Bridges and Sam Aiston as exciting prospects for the not too distant future gave Reid the luxury and satisfaction of being able to nurture a wealth of home grown talent.

Two of the season's most astute moves involved the loan signing of Blackburn Rovers' third choice goalkeeper Shay Given and the free transfer capture of Liverpool's England international Paul Stewart, initially on loan but with a view to a permanent move.

Not even early elimination from both domestic cup competitions could detract from Sunderland's magnificent season. A first round tie in the League Cup paired Sunderland with Preston North End. A 1-1 draw at Deepdale was followed by a 3-2 success at Roker Park to set up a mouth-watering encounter with the mighty Liverpool. Although Sunderland lost both the away and home games in the two-legged tie by 2-0 and 1-0 respectively, an early measure of Sunderland's progress was that they were far from outplayed by their more illustrious opponents and most neutral observers felt that the 2-0 scoreline at Anfield did not do Sunderland justice. In the F.A. Cup, Sunderland gave Manchester United the fright of their lives as they stormed into a 2-1 lead at Old Trafford with goals from Agnew and Russell. The game ended 2-2 with Alex Ferguson admitting "We were the luckiest team in the world to get a replay." In the replay at Roker Park, Phil Gray scored to give Sunderland a half-time lead and although Manchester United ran out eventual 2-1 winners, Sunderland could hold their heads high.

**Incoming players included:**
Paul Bracewell, Gareth Hall, David Kelly, John Mullin

**Outgoing players included:**
Shaun Cunnington, Derek Ferguson, Tony Norman, Ian Rodgerson, Anthony Smith.

*Note: Throughout this book the names of players included in the 'incoming players' listings has been restricted to those players who were under permanent contract. Loan players are not included.*

**Sunderland's league record read:-**

| P | W | D | L | F | A | Pts | Position |
|---|---|---|---|---|---|-----|----------|
| 46 | 22 | 17 | 7 | 59 | 33 | 83 | 1st |

League appearances (with F.A. Cup and League Cup appearances in brackets): Agnew 26 (2), Aiston 4, Angell 2 (1), Atkinson 5 (3), Ball 35 (5), Bracewell 38 (6), Bridges 2, Chamberlain 29 (6), Cook 6, Given 17, Gray (Martin) 4 (1), Gray (Michael) 46 (6), Gray (Phil) 28 (6), Hall 8, Howey 17 (1), Kelly 9 (2), Kubicki 46 (6), Melville 40 (4), Mullin 5 (1), Ord 41 (5), Russell 35 (3), Scott 43 (5), Smith 9 (3), Stewart 11.

Average home attendance: 17,500

*Paul Bracewell was Peter Reid's first signing prior to the start of the 1995-1996 season.*

*On the day of Sunderland's confirmed promotion to the Premiership, Peter Reid told the Sports Echo, "Without a doubt this is as good as any moment I have enjoyed in football. A year ago we finished with 54 points and we were nearly relegated. I don't think anybody in their right minds would look a year on and see Sunderland Football Club in this position. I thought we would go near to the play-offs. We have to be realistic because we have done it without the injured Martin Smith, David Kelly and Phil Gray for a fair bit of this season." Reid identified the start of Sunderland's renaissance as being 17th February 1996 when Lee Howey rescued Sunderland at Portsmouth with an injury team headed equaliser. That goal sparked an amazing run of results which culminated in the winning of the First Division Championship! "I cannot stress just how important that goal was," said Peter Reid.*

**During the 1995/1996 season Sunderland's amazing run of results included:—**

● **Nine consecutive league wins. This created a post war record.**

● **An unbeaten run of eighteen league games. This created an all-time record.**

● **Twenty six league games with clean sheets. This created a post war record.**

● **Only seven league defeats. This represented the fewest league defeats in a season since the 1963-1964 season.**

● **Craig Russell became one of only seven Sunderland players to score four or more goals in a game during post war years.**

# COUNTDOWN TO THE PREMIERSHIP

**Date: 12th August 1995**

**Result:** SUNDERLAND 1 LEICESTER CITY 2

Sunderland scorer(s): **Agnew**      Attendance: 18,593

Verdict: Relegated Leicester City emphasised the difference in class between the Premiership and the First Division as they gave Sunderland a lesson in controlled football for virtually the entire game. Bracewell was outstanding in midfield but with the visitors' defence in command, Leicester's goalkeeper was rarely tested.

**League position: 21st**

---

**Date: 19th August 1995**

**Result:** NORWICH CITY 0 SUNDERLAND 0

Attendance: 16,739

Verdict: The Sunderland defence was under pressure in the early stages but, as the game progressed, Sunderland had their fair share of possession with Howey and Ord both unlucky not to score. A heartening performance by Sunderland against one of the early season promotion favourites.

**League position: 21st**

---

**Date: 26th August 1995**

**Result:** SUNDERLAND 2 WOLVERHAMPTON WANDERERS 0

Sunderland scorer(s): **P. Gray, Melville**      Attendance: 16,816

Verdict: Sunderland completely outplayed the most expensively assembled team in the First Division. Wolves were never given the chance to show their obvious skills and Sunderland could have had an avalanche of goals as they repeatedly surged forward in a one sided game.

**League position: 15th**

---

**Date: 29th August 1995**

**Result:** PORT VALE 1 SUNDERLAND 1

Sunderland scorer(s): **P. Gray**      Attendance: 7,693

Verdict: After conceding a second minute goal, Sunderland hit back in convincing style and should have gone on to win the game. Craig Russell had two good chances in as many minutes, although Chamberlain was called on to make two great saves.

**League position: 14th**

---

**Date: 2nd September 1995**

**Result:** IPSWICH TOWN 3 SUNDERLAND 0

Attendance: 12,390

Verdict: A misleading scoreline with Sunderland in total control throughout the first half. They paid the penalty for not accepting a string of first half chances and Ipswich stormed into a 2-0 lead by half-time. In the second half, both Craig Russell and Phil Gray missed good chances before Mathie completed his hat-trick, against the run of play. Sam Aiston came on in the second half and made an encouraging debut.

**League position: 19th**

---

**Date: 9th September 1995**

**Result:** SUNDERLAND 1 SOUTHEND UNITED 0

Sunderland scorer(s): **Russell**      Attendance: 13,805

Verdict: Sunderland played better at Ipswich the previous week and lost. They found it very difficult to cope with Southend's tight marking and one of the few bright spots of the game was Russell's magnificent solo goal. Kevin Ball was sent off but Southend were unable to take advantage of having the extra man.

**League position: 15th**

---

**Date: 12th September 1995**

**Result:** SUNDERLAND 1 PORTSMOUTH 1

Sunderland scorer(s): **Melville**      Attendance: 12,282

Verdict: A disappointing performance. After scoring on 6 minutes, Sunderland squandered several chances including a penalty miss by Phil Gray, only for Portsmouth to level the scores from the penalty spot four minutes from time. It was a particularly frustrating night for Phil Gray and the crowd's chant of 'There's only one Chris Waddle' said it all.

**League position: 15th**

**Date: 16th September 1995**

**Result:** LUTON TOWN 0    SUNDERLAND 2

Sunderland scorer(s): **P. Gray, Mullin**        Attendance 6,955

Verdict: After a fairly even first half, Sunderland put on a powerful second half display to run out easy winners. With the defence rarely tested, Sunderland could even afford the luxury of a missed Phil Gray penalty.

**League position: 9th**

---

**Date: 23rd September 1995**

**Result:** MILLWALL 1    SUNDERLAND 2

Sunderland scorer(s): **Scott, Smith**        Attendance: 8,691

Verdict: The score did not do justice to Sunderland's enterprising play against their high flying opponents. An extremely convincing performance in which Michael Gray and John Mullin were outstanding.

**League position: 7th**

---

**Date: 30th September 1995**

**Result:** SUNDERLAND 2    READING 2

Sunderland scorer(s): **Kelly, Melville**        Attendance: 17,503

Verdict: An entertaining game in which both sides had lots of chances. After dominating the game for long spells, Sunderland had to wait until the 89th minute for the equaliser.

**League position: 6th**

---

**Date: 7th October 1995**

**Result:** CRYSTAL PALACE 0    SUNDERLAND 1

Sunderland scorer(s): **Kelly**        Attendance 13,754

Verdict: Sunderland were at their best in the first half and although Crystal Palace increased their share of possession in the second half the Sunderland defence held tight. After Sunderland missed another two penalties (Scott and Bracewell), it looked as if the game was heading for a goalless draw when Kelly pounced in the 75th minute.

**League position: 3rd**

---

**Date: 14th October 1995**

**Result:** SUNDERLAND 1    WATFORD 1

Sunderland scorer(s): **Scott**        Attendance: 17,790

Verdict: A superb display by the Watford goalkeeper prevented Sunderland recording a landslide win. Sunderland controlled most of a very entertaining game and deserved to have more than a cracking goal from Martin Scott to show for their efforts.

**League position: 4th**

---

**Date: 21st October 1995**

**Result:** HUDDERSFIELD TOWN 1    SUNDERLAND 1

Sunderland scorer(s): **P. Gray**        Attendance: 16,054

Verdict: Although not at their best, Sunderland were on top for long spells and it was an injustice when Huddersfield took the lead. Sunderland missed several chances and looked most dangerous on the wings where Sam Aiston and Michael Gray were in good form.

**League position: 5th**

---

**Date: 28th October 1995**

**Result:** SUNDERLAND 2    BARNSLEY 1

Sunderland scorer(s): **Howey, Russell**        Attendance: 17,024

Verdict: Sunderland had to work hard for this victory. From the start, Russell ran the Barnsley defence ragged and but for a first half injury he could have contributed to a more convincing win. After Barnsely had pulled one goal back, Sunderland were forced on to the defensive and hung on grimly to claim all three points. Substitute Sam Aiston once again impressed.

**League position: 5th**

---

**Date: 5th November 1995**

**Result:** CHARLTON ATHLETIC 1    SUNDERLAND 1

Sunderland scorer(s): **Michael Gray**        Attendance: 11,626

Verdict: Sunderland's acute goalscoring problems were broadcast by the television cameras. This was a game which Sunderland could have easily won if Phil Gray and David Kelly had not been guilty of two glaring misses. Star man Michael Gray scored the only goal of the game but the worry for Sunderland had to be that neither Kelly nor Phil Gray had a single shot on target.

**League position: 4th**

**Date: 18th November 1995**

**Result: SUNDERLAND 2    SHEFFIELD UNITED 0**

Sunderland scorer(s): **Phil Gray (2)**          Attendance 16,640

Verdict: The Yorkshire team's bustling tactics completely knocked Sunderland out of their stride for the first hour. The visitors had few attacking ideas and rarely looked capable of snatching a win so a draw seemed to be the most likely outcome until two lethal strikes from Phil Gray settled the issue in Sunderland's favour.

**League position: 4th**

---

**Date: 22nd November 1995**

**Result: STOKE CITY 1    SUNDERLAND 0**

Attendance: 11,754

Verdict: A double blow for Sunderland with a first league defeat in twelve games and the loss of Paul Bracewell through injury. Following Bracewell's withdrawal, Sunderland showed very little inventive play and rarely looked capable of forcing an equaliser. They paid the price for early missed chances by Phil Gray, Russell and Kelly.

**League position: 7th**

---

**Date: 25th November 1995**

**Result: WEST BROM. ALBION 0    SUNDERLAND 1**

Sunderland scorer(s): **Howey**          Attendance: 15,931

Verdict: Lee Howey's superb header was the only time that Sunderland seriously threatened Albion's goal. Alec Chamberlain produced two good saves and the central defence pairing of Ord and Melville was outstanding as the Midlands side increased the pace of the game as they searched for the equaliser.

**League position: 6th**

---

**Date: 3rd December 1995**

**Result: SUNDERLAND 1    CRYSTAL PALACE 0**

Sunderland scorer(s): **Scott**          Attendance: 12,777

Verdict: Sunderland's first 'double' of the season. A game where the result was more rewarding than the performance. Sunderland displayed few attacking ideas and failed to produce a single clear cut chance in the first half. It was not surprising that a game in which neither side looked capable of scoring should be settled with a penalty. Star players for Sunderland were Ball, Ord and Chamberlain.

**League position: 2nd**

---

**Date: 9th December 1995**

**Result: SUNDERLAND 6    MILLWALL 0**

Sunderland scorer(s): **P. Gray, Russell (4), Scott**  Attendance: 18,951

Verdict: Rampant Sunderland pushed the previous leaders aside and hit them for six. The visitors were totally outplayed as Sunderland's attack finally gelled and produced a magnificent display of football.

**League position: 1st**

---

**Date: 16th December 1995**

**Result: READING 1    SUNDERLAND 1**

Sunderland scorer(s): **Smith**          Attendance: 9,431

Verdict: Sunderland were well on top over the ninety minutes and looked in a different class to Reading. After going a goal ahead, Sunderland lacked the killer instinct to wrap the game up and were left counting the cost when Reading player/manager Jimmy Quinn forced home an equaliser in the 86th minute.

**League position: 1st**

---

**Date: 23rd December 1995**

**Result: DERBY COUNTY 3    SUNDERLAND 1**

Sunderland scorer(s): **Michael Gray**          Attendance: 16,882

Verdict: Sunderland played well enough to come away from the Baseball Ground with at least a point. Two disputed goals by Derby produced a final score which flattered them.

**League position: 2nd**

---

**Date: 14th January 1996**

**Result: SUNDERLAND 0    NORWICH CITY 1**

Attendance: 14,983

Verdict: After a three week lay-off due to bad weather, Sunderland produced a below par performance. David Kelly left the field after two minutes with a serious injury but this was no excuse for such a lack lustre effort. They had four clear cut chances over the ninety minutes but could not place one on target. Anxiety set in as the team ran out of attacking ideas to salvage a point.

**League position: 8th**

**Date: 21st January 1996**

**Result:** | **LEICESTER CITY 0   SUNDERLAND 0**

Attendance 16,130

Verdict: The high spots for Sunderland were in defence where Melville, Scott and Kubicki held a tight grip on the game from start to finish while Shay Given made an impressive debut in goal. Sunderland began to push forward more in the second half when both Russell and Phil Gray squandered several opportunties.

**League position: 7th**

---

**Date: 24th January 1996**

**Result:** | **SUNDERLAND 1   GRIMSBY TOWN 0**

Sunderland scorer(s): **Ord**          Attendance: 14,656

Verdict; A dreadful game which further emphasised Sunderland's lack of strike power. Another competent defensive display but the lack of ideas up front made a mockery of Sunderland's claims to be serious promotion contenders.

**League position: 4th**

---

**Date: 30th January 1996**

**Result:** | **SUNDERLAND 0   TRANMERE ROVERS 0**

Attendance: 17,616

Verdict: With five players out of the side through injury, Peter Reid was forced to shuffle the team's paper thin squad. Lee Howey was moved back into central defence and gave a good account of himself. Tranmere Rovers had lost several of their recent matches and came to Roker to frustrate Sunderland. Both sides could look back on missed chances but Sunderland's lack of attacking options were once again the main talking point.

**League position: 3rd**

---

**Date: 3rd February 1996**

**Result:** | **WOLVERHAMPTON WANDERERS 3 SUNDERLAND 0**

Attendance: 26,537

Verdict: Humiliation in the Midlands as Sunderland's makeshift side were torn apart by Wolves. In complete contrast to the meeting between the two clubs at Roker Park earlier in the season, the Rokermen's lightweight attack made no impression. After an extremely disappointing first half, Sunderland did increase their share of possession after the break but they never looked like scoring.

**League position: 5th**

---

**Date: 10th February 1996**

**Result:** | **SUNDERLAND 0   PORT VALE 0**

Attendance: 15,954

Verdict: A game of two defences. Sunderland's back four had little difficulty in coping with Port Vale's few attacking moves but with the Potteries side setting their sights no higher than a point, the visitor's defence was given few problems by a Sunderland attack who were woefully short of ideas in front of goal.

**League position: 5th**

---

**Date: 17th February 1996**

**Result:** | **PORTSMOUTH 2   SUNDERLAND 2**

Sunderland scorer(s): **Agnew, Howey**      Attendance: 12,241

Verdict: A tactical move by Peter Reid saw Phil Gray dropped from the side with Agnew drafted in to strengthen the midfield and Russell left alone up front. Sunderland took a deserved lead through Agnew early in the game but when Portsmouth scored their second goal on 86 minutes it looked as if the Rokermen would be leaving empty handed. Howey's powerful header in injury time gave Sunderland a deserved share of the spoils.

**League position: 5th**

---

**Date: 20th February 1996**

**Result:** | **SUNDERLAND 1   IPSWICH TOWN 0**

Sunderland scorer(s): **Russell**          Attendance: 14,052

Verdict: At Portman Road in September, Sunderland overran Ipswich for long periods of the game only to loose by a misleading 3-0 scoreline. Here, Ipswich completely outplayed and outclassed Sunderland in a first half in which Sunderland struggled to string two passes together. Despite the visitors' dominance, they failed to convert a string of first half chances while Sunderland's one shot on target resulted in the only goal of the game.

**League position: 3rd**

---

**Date: 24th February 1996**

**Result:** | **SUNDERLAND 1   LUTON TOWN 0**

Sunderland scorer(s): **James** (own goal)   Attendance: 16,693

Verdict: Sunderland needed to dig deep to grind out this result in a dour game. Luton surged forward in spells but as usual Sunderland's defence held firm. Kevin Ball gave a five star performance in midfield.

**League position: 3rd**

**Date: 27th February 1996**

Result: **SOUTHEND UNITED 0   SUNDERLAND 2**

Sunderland scorer(s): **Bridges, Scott**          Attendance: 5,786

Verdict: Sunderland's game plan appeared to be to stifle the home side's attack in the first half and to rely on the quick break forward. A goal up at half time, Sunderland took control of the game in the second half and could have won by a much bigger margin. After some indifferent performances at home, Michael Gray was back to his sizzling best in this game.

**League position: 2nd**

---

**Date: 3rd March 1996**

Result: **GRIMSBY TOWN 0   SUNDERLAND 4**

Sunderland scorer(s): **Ball, Bridges, P. Gray, Russell** Attendance: 5,318

Verdict: The scoreline may have flattered Sunderland but there was no doubting the fact that Peter Reid's men were in a different class to the home team. Sunderland playing with a new found confidence, controlled the game from start to finish.

**League position: 2nd**

---

**Date: 9th March 1996**

Result: **SUNDERLAND 3   DERBY COUNTY 0**

Sunderland scorer(s): **Agnew, Russell (2)**   Attendance: 21,644

Verdict: This was billed as the First Division's match of the season and was expected to be a closely fought encounter between the two top placed sides. On the day, Derby were blitzed by a Sunderland team firing on all cylinders and had no answer to the electrifying pace of the Rokermen's forwards. Despite an obvious lack of match fitness, Paul Stewart showed himself to be a class act and such was the dominance of the Sunderland defence that goalkeeper Shay Given had to wait until the 84th minute to make his first real save of the game.

**League position: 2nd**

---

**Date: 12th March 1996**

Result: **OLDHAM ATHLETIC 1   SUNDERLAND 2**

Sunderland scorer(s): **Ball, Michael Gray**    Attendance: 7,149

Verdict: After five successive clean sheets, Sunderland were stunned to concede a goal! An opportunist lob by Michael Gray and a powerful header by Ball from a free kick secured all three points for Sunderland to underline their promotion credentials.

**League position: 2nd**

---

**Date: 17th March 1996**

Result: **BIRMINGHAM 0   SUNDERLAND 2**

Sunderland scorer(s): **Agnew, Melville**   Attendance: 23,251

Verdict: With the promotion bandwagon now in overdrive, Sunderland produced a solid workmanlike performance in all departments and moved the ball around with all the self assurance of a team expecting to come out on top. Ball and Bracewell ran the show from midfield and, with Sunderland in control of the game, Shay Given had just one save to make all afternoon.

**League position: 1st**

---

**Date: 23rd March 1996**

Result: **SUNDERLAND 1   OLDHAM ATHLETIC 0**

Sunderland scorer(s) **Scott**          Attendance: 20,631

Verdict: Win number eight on the trot and the best winning sequence this century. This was the least convincing performance of the run. With Oldham packing their defence in search of a point, Sunderland were restricted to just two long range shots, one apiece from Scott and Bracewell, in a dour first half. Sunderland failed to get going in the second half with only a shot from Craig Russell to raise the crowd's spirits. Martin Scott settled the issue in the 82nd minute but even then it took a breathtaking save from Shay Given to deny Oldham a point.

**League position: 1st**

---

**Date: 30th March 1996**

Result: **SUNDERLAND 3 HUDDERSFIELD TOWN 2**

Sunderland scorer(s): **Ball, Bridges (2)** Attendance: 20,131

Verdict: What a difference a year makes! This game marked Peter Reid's first year in charge at Roker and extended Sunderland's winning run to nine games. Twice Sunderland were a goal down but each time the team's new found confidence and self belief won the day as they fought back with goals from Kevin Ball and super-sub Michael Bridges whose two magnificent headers in a four minute spell against a Huddersfield side reduced to ten men capped a sensational twelve months of Peter Reid leadership.

**League position: 1st**

---

**Date: 2nd April 1996**

Result: **WATFORD 3   SUNDERLAND 3**

Sunderland scorer(s): **Agnew, Ball, Russell**   Attendance: 11,195

Verdict: Despite three well taken first half goals by Sunderland, uncharacteristic defensive errors cost the Rokermen a tenth consecutive victory over basement club Watford. Sunderland twice had the cushion of a two goal lead but the normally commanding defence fell apart as Watford surged forward in the second half.

**League position: 1st**

**Date: 6th April 1996**

**Result:** **BARNSLEY 0    SUNDERLAND 1**

Sunderland scorer(s): **Russell**          Attendance: 13,189

Verdict: Over 7,000 Sunderland fans made the trip to Oakwell to see the Rokermen stretch their unbeaten run to thirteen games. Russell put Sunderland ahead after 24 minutes when he turned to force home a Michael Gray corner. Following Paul Stewart's dismissal just before half time, ten man Sunderland mounted a battling rearguard action for the entire second half.

**League position: 1st**

---

**Date: 16th April 1996**

**Result:** **SUNDERLAND 3 BIRMINGHAM CITY 0**

Sunderland scorer(s): **Michael Gray, Stewart, Russell**   Attendance: 19,831

Verdict: A thoroughly professional performance by Sunderland overwhelmed Barry Fry's team. The atmosphere at Roker Park was electric as Sunderland stormed into a 2-0 lead after 21 minutes following a stunning thirty yard shot by Michael Gray and a header by Paul Stewart. Craig Russell kept his cool as he side-stepped the goalkeeper to add a third in the second half to cap a superb all-round team effort by Sunderland to virtually guarantee promotion.

**League position: 1st**

---

**Date: 8th April 1996**

**Result:** **SUNDERLAND 0  CHARLTON ATHLETIC 0**

Attendance: 20,914

Verdict: Shay Given and Craig Russell were both ruled out of this game through injury. Sunderland missed Russell's hard running and mounted only a handful of attacks all afternoon. Chamberlain made an excellent save during a rare Charlton attack and although the Rokermen pressed forward in the latter stages of the game, this was Sunderland's least convincing performance for some time.

**League position: 1st**

---

**Date: 21st April 1996**

**Result:** **SUNDERLAND 0    STOKE CITY 0**

Attendance: 21,276

Verdict: With promotion already assured, Sunderland needed to win this one to guarantee the championship but they found it hard going against a gritty Stoke side. Ord volleyed over from six yards out and substitute Bridges shaved a post but chances were few and far between with the Potteries side setting out their stall for a point.

**League position: 1st**

---

**Date: 13th April 1996**

**Result:** **SHEFFIELD UNITED 0  SUNDERLAND 0**

Attendance: 20,050

Verdict: An end-to-end game with few clear-cut chances. Alec Chamberlain saved well from United's Andy Walker in the early stages while the hard running Craig Russell had an effort cleared off the line. Michael Gray tantalised the home side's defence for most of the game while Kevin Ball had another solid game in midfield.

**League position: 1st**

---

**Date: 27th April 1996**

**Result:** **SUNDERLAND 0  WEST BROM. ALBION 0**

Attendance: 22,027

Verdict: It was carnival time at Roker Park as promoted Sunderland chased the one point they needed to clinch the championship. In the early stages it looked as if Peter Reid's men were going to run riot as Russell, Agnew and Howey all failed to convert good chances. With the inspirational Kevin Ball missing through suspension, Sunderland began to loose their way in the second half and although Albion rarely threatened the Sunderland goal, Chamberlain came to Sunderland's rescue with a point blank save from Burgess.

**League position: 1st**

---

**Date: 5th May 1996**

**Result:** **TRANMERE ROVERS  2        SUNDERLAND   0**

Attendance: 16,193

Verdict: With the influential Paul Bracewell and key defender Andy Melville missing, Sunderland fielded a re-shuffled side. Bridges and Russell had both missed good early chances before the home team took the lead against the run of play. In the second half, Ord had a shot saved and an effort from Ball was cleared off the line. Tranmere sealed their victory via a disputed penalty to send Sunderland crashing to their first defeat in nineteen games.

**League position: 1st**

*A determined gesture by Peter Reid on the day of his first match in charge at Roker Park.*

*First Division Champions 1995-1996.*

*Michael Gray was an ever-present during the 1995-1996 season.*

*Left back Martin Scott scored some crucial goals for Sunderland during the championship season including the one against Oldham Athletic in Sunderland's 1–0 win at Roker Park.*

*Peter Reid's first signing at Sunderland was Paul Bracewell who joined the club for the third time before the start of the 1995-1996 season.*

*Craig Russell's goals played a major part in helping Sunderland lift the First Division championship. Four of his goals came in the 6–0
trouncing of Millwall at Roker Park on 9th December 1995.*

*Darius Kubicki has made the number two shirt his own since moving to Sunderland from Aston Villa. Polish international.*

*Steve Agnew's goals and tantalising crosses contributed to Sunderland's success story.*

*Welsh international Andy Melville formed a formidable partnership with Richard Ord at the heart of the Sunderland defence.*

*Martin Smith, one of Sunderland's most exciting prospects, missed several games during the second half of the championship season through injury.*

*Lee Howey's versatility was demonstrated when he started games in both attack and defence during the 1995-1996 season.*

*Shay Given who joined Sunderland on loan from Blackburn Rovers proved to be one of Peter Reid's most astute signings of his managerial career.*

*Skipper Kevin Ball whose contribution to Sunderland's success cannot be overestimated.*

*Seventeen-year-old Michael Bridges whose crucial goals earned him super-sub status during the promotion season.*

*The party starts here! Sunderland players celebrate their winning of the First Division Championship after the home game against West Bromwich Albion.*

# POST WAR FACTS

## Honours

| | | |
|---|---|---|
| Division 2 | Runners Up | 1963/1964 |
| Division 2 | Champions | 1975/1976 |
| Division 2 | Runners Up | 1979/1980 |
| Division 3 | Champions | 1987/1988 |
| Division 1 | Champions | 1995/1996 |
| | | |
| F.A. Cup | Winners | 1973 |
| F.A. Cup | Runners Up | 1992 |
| | | |
| Football League Cup | Runners Up | 1985 |

## Highest Home Attendances

| | | | |
|---|---|---|---|
| League | 68,004 v | Newcastle United | 1949/1950 |
| F.A. Cup | 65,125 v | Norwich City | 1950/1951 |
| Football League Cup | 38,975 v | Derby County | 1973/1974 |

## Lowest Home Attendances

| | | | |
|---|---|---|---|
| League | 7,469 v | Cardiff City | 1952/1953 |
| F.A. Cup | 12,352 v | Newport County | 1985/1986 |
| Football League Cup | 8,161 v | Huddersfield Town | 1991/1992 |

## Record Victories

| | | | | |
|---|---|---|---|---|
| Sunderland | 8 | Charlton Athletic | 1 | 1956/1957 |
| Sunderland | 7 | Southend United | 0 | 1987/1988 |

## Record Defeats

| | | | | |
|---|---|---|---|---|
| West Ham United | 8 | Sunderland | 0 | 1968/1969 |
| Watford | 8 | Sunderland | 0 | 1982/1983 |

## Sunderland players to score four or more goals in a game:

| | | | |
|---|---|---|---|
| Robinson | 4 v | Blackpool | 1946/1947 |
| Turnbull | 4 v | Portsmouth | 1947/1948 |
| Ford | 4 v | Manchester City | 1952/1953 |
| Sharkey | 5 v | Norwich City | 1962/1963 |
| Cummins | 4 v | Burnley | 1979/1980 |
| Gates | 4 v | Southend United | 1987/1988 |
| Russell | 4 v | Millwall | 1995/1996 |

# PROMOTIONS
## and
# RELEGATIONS

Over the years Sunderland and its supporters have had more than their fair share of false dawns. The current successful promotion campaign is the fifth occasion that Sunderland have regained top flight soccer status and each time the achievement has been accompanied by empty words of optimism for the future.

Sunderland's first promotion was secured during the 1963-1964 season with Alan Brown at the helm. It took Brown six seasons to restore the Rokermen's top flight status after he himself had presided over the team's shock relegation in 1957-1958 for the first time in the club's history. Despite Brown's much talked-about youth policy and the board's promise of cash injections for team strengthening, Alan Brown walked out on the club during the close season and the club dithered for several months before appointing George Hardwick as caretaker manager. Hardwick received a pittance for transfer activity and the impetus of promotion was dissipated.

When Sunderland were relegated in 1969-1970 as an inevitable consequence of inadequate investment, it took the club and the Messiah Bob Stokoe six and three seasons respectively to win the old Second Division Championship. Nine games into the new season, Stokoe asked to be relieved of his duties. The club were relegated at the conclusion of its first season back in the big time.

After four years of Second Division football, Ken Knighton was appointed manager and immediately led Sunderland to promotion, thanks to the inheritance of a strong team and significant finances. However a string of poor results in his first season in the top flight and an uneasy working relationship with club chairman Tom Cowie contributed to Knighton's dismissal.

Sunderland's fourth promotion to the premier league was fortuitous, to say the least. Denis Smith rescued Sunderland from the wastelands of the old Third Division, and in his third season in charge, took the club to the Second Division Play-Off Final and a Wembley appearance. Smith's team were outclassed by Swindon Town, losing 1-0, but were nevertheless promoted thanks to a decision by the Football League to punish the Wiltshire club for earlier financial irregularities. Sunderland AFC's failure to cash-in on their good fortune in the naive belief that a team which had finished in sixth position in a mediocre Second Division would be good enough to hold its own amongst the elite of English soccer, virtually rubber stamped a swift return to the lower echelons. Smith was sacked and thereafter followed a succession of internally appointed managers who collectively almost condemned Sunderland to a second and possibly longer spell of third rate soccer.

With the possible exception of Bob Stokoe's fairytale F.A. Cup success of 1973, Peter Reid's magnificent feat in leading Sunderland back to their rightful place at the pinnacle of English football exceeds every achievement of the past fifty years at the club. With the club now about to re-locate to a magnificent new stadium which it is claimed will be the best in the country, it is imperative that the board learns from its previous shortsighted mistakes and makes significant sums of cash available to Peter Reid for team strengthening to ensure that Premiership status is preserved.

# SUPPORTERS TO THE LIMITED EDITION

1. Mr Stuart D. Bell
2. Mr Keith Metcalfe
3. Mr David L. Dodds
4. Mr Paul Healey
5. Mr Mark J. Dorrian
6. Miss Alexandra C. Bayley-Kaye
7. Mr Trevor Wood
8. Mr Geoff Dickens
9. Mrs Val Waistell
10. Mr C. Reynolds
11. Mr T. Gibson
12. Mr R. Eagleton
13. Mr Colin W. Smith
14. Mrs Patricia Snowdon
15. Mr John G. Hellens
16. Mr W. U. Bell
17. Mr Stephen Graham
18. Mr Ian Crossley
19. Mr Paul Killan
20. Mr Anthony Waites
21. Mr Graeme Sussmilch
22. Mr Michael Beech
23. Mr G. Lavery
24. Mr Gerry Rutter
25. Mrs Joan Banks
26. Mr Rowland Mizen
27. Mr Stanley Smith
28. Mr David Smith
29. Mrs Joan Tate
30. Mrs Marie Yates
31. Mr John Tennet
32. Mr Jim D. Stokoe
33. Mr Anthony Stephenson
34. Mr Ron Scott
35. Mr Gareth Pearson
36. Mr Bernard Duncan
37. Mr Paul Lindley
38. Mr Peter Whitfield
39. Mr William Whitfield
40. Mr James Cairns
41. Mr Gordon White
42. Mr Ian Powell
43. Mr Keith Tarn
44. Mr William Price
45. Mr Alan Stewart
46. Mr John Said
47. Mr Robert Cowe Jnr.
48. Mrs Judith Mawby
49. Mr Paul Spiteri
50. Mr John Trotter
51. Mr Michael Lowes
52. Mr Alan Coats
53. Mr Jack Dunn
54. Mr Andrew McKenzie
55. Mr Michael Flaherty
56. Mr Mark Musgrave
57. Mr Shaun Musgrave
58. Mr Fennick-Pearson Hunnam
59. Mr John R. Dent
60. Mr Michael C. Hickey
61. Mr Kevin Welsh
62. Mr Alan Slater
63. Mr Arthur Campbell
64. Mr Bill Hern
65. Mr Len Atkinson
66. Mr Scott Phillips
67. Miss Debbie Malloy
68. Mr James Alexander
69. Mr Keith Ayre
70. Mr Keith Cockerill
71. Rev. David Tweddle
72. Mr John Fawcett
73. Mr Cyril Bond
74. Mr David Ratcliffe
75. Mr Peter Connor
76. Mr Roy Mills
77. Mr Alan Young
78. Mr Matthew Scott
79. Mr John Colman
80. Mr W. K. Robinson
81. Mr Mark Citrone
82. Mr Tony Citrone
83. Mr Tony Gavin Jnr.
84. Mr W. R. Strong
85. Mr Brian Morrison
86. Mr Adam Treweeke
87. Mr John Pallister
88. Mr Tony Weatherill
89. Mr Dennis Rodgers
90. Mr Ian Barker
91. Mr Alan Nicklas
92. Mr Ray White
93. Mr Ron Dixon
94. Mr Alan Lee
95. Mr Frank Cook
96. Mr Paul Dowson
97. Mr James Hill
98. Mr Ian Mills
99. Mr Sakari Mononen
100. Mr John Surtees
101. Mr John Surtees
102. Mr John Kitchin
103. Mr Colin Dunn
104. Mr James Duffy
105. Mr Andrew Cockburn
106. Mr Jeffrey Jameson
107. Mr Fred Bage
108. Mr Roger Mason
109. Mr John King
110. Mr George Wright
111. Mr Michael Craggs
112. Mr Carlo Plows
113. Mr Ken Cheal
114. Mr Graham Lowen
115. Mr Scott Hagan
116. Mr Stan Sharp
117. Mr David Scott
118. Mr Bill Fisher
119. Mr Bob Gurney
120. Mr Tony Lawson
121. Mr K. J. Fitzgeraid
122. Mr David Taylor
123. Mr Alan Thynne
124. Mr Andrew Hair
125. Mr John Rafter
126. Mr Richard Stevens
127. Mr Keith Goodwin
128. Mr Paul Scott
129. Mr Kevin Webster
130. Mr Peter Hair
131. Miss Christine Kelly
132. Mr Stephen Downes
133. Mr Thomas Thompkins
134. Mr Brian Doyle
135. Mr Mark Dixon
136. Mr William Kennedy
137. Mr Darryl McColl
138. Mr Steven Bell
139. Mr Derek Bell
140. Mr Ian Taylor
141. Mr David Plumpton
142. Mr Keith Green
143. Mr Jimmy Traynor
144. Mr Peter Harris
145. Mr Paul Tinkler
146. Mr Ron Smith
147. Mr Christopher Pattinson
148. Mrs Valerie Clark
149. Mr John Clark
150. Mr Jack Clark

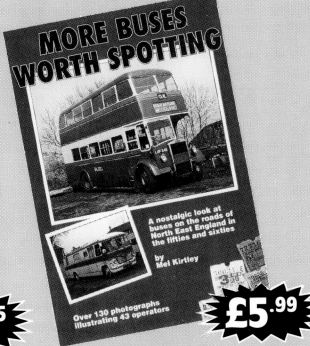

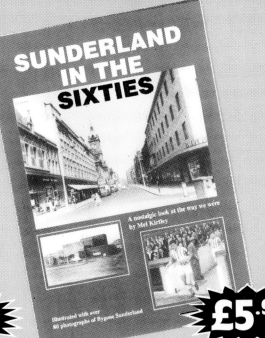